FIRST
GIVING GOD FIRST PLACE

Pastor Ikenna Okeke

authorHOUSE

AuthorHouse™ UK
1663 Liberty Drive
Bloomington, IN 47403 USA
www.authorhouse.co.uk
Phone: 0800 047 8203 (Domestic TFN)
      +44 1908 723714 (International)

© 2019 Pastor Ikenna Okeke. All rights reserved.

No part of this book may be reproduced, stored in a retrieval system, or transmitted by any means without the written permission of the author.

Published by AuthorHouse 06/17/2019

ISBN: 978-1-7283-8961-5 (sc)
ISBN: 978-1-7283-8962-2 (hc)
ISBN: 978-1-7283-8960-8 (e)

Print information available on the last page.

Any people depicted in stock imagery provided by Getty Images are models, and such images are being used for illustrative purposes only.
Certain stock imagery © Getty Images.

This book is printed on acid-free paper.

Because of the dynamic nature of the Internet, any web addresses or links contained in this book may have changed since publication and may no longer be valid. The views expressed in this work are solely those of the author and do not necessarily reflect the views of the publisher, and the publisher hereby disclaims any responsibility for them.

Scripture quotations marked NKJV are taken from the New King James Version. Copyright © 1982 by Thomas Nelson, Inc. Used by permission. All rights reserved.

Scripture quotations marked MSG are taken from THE MESSAGE. Copyright © 1993, 1994, 1995, 1996, 2000, 2001, 2002, 2003 by Eugene H. Peterson. Used by permission of NavPress Publishing Group. Website.

Scripture quotations marked KJV are from the Holy Bible, King James Version (Authorized Version). First published in 1611. Quoted from the KJV Classic Reference Bible, Copyright © 1983 by The Zondervan Corporation.

The Easy-to-Read Version (ERV) is an English translation of the Bible by the World Bible Translation Center (WBTC), a subsidiary of Bible League International. It was originally published as the English Version for the Deaf (EVD) by BakerBooks. Copyright © 2006 by Bible League international

Contents

Acknowledgements vii
Introduction ix

Chapter 1	His Rightful Place 1
Chapter 2	100% Saved! 7
Chapter 3	Follow the Cloud 10
Chapter 4	Change Your Diet 19
Chapter 5	Eat of the Tree of Life 23
Chapter 6	If God Be for Us 29
Chapter 7	The Promisor, the Promise, and the Conditions 36
Chapter 8	Chosen for Success 41
Chapter 9	In the Name of Jesus 50
Chapter 10	The True Disciple 55
Chapter 11	Genuine Witnesses 59
Chapter 12	Depend on God 65
Chapter 13	Enjoy What You Have 70
Chapter 14	Embrace Your Calling 74
Chapter 15	The Principle of Mercy Problems 78
Chapter 16	Camouflage of Blessing 82
Chapter 17	Where Have You Laid Him? 88
Chapter 18	Accurately Waiting on God 90
Chapter 19	God Will Not Forget 92
Chapter 20	Increasing Faith—By Reason of Use 99
Chapter 21	The Technology of Faith 103
Chapter 22	Faith Ignores Circumstance 106
Chapter 23	Contrary to Evidence 110
Chapter 24	I Am Not Home Yet 114

Chapter 25   The Rights of the Believer 123
Chapter 26   The Necessity of Confrontation 127
Chapter 27   The Weapons of Our Warfare 130
Chapter 28   Winning Your Battles 134
Chapter 29   God's Love in Action 138
Chapter 30   Looking through the Eyes of the Cross 141
Chapter 31   Thanksgiving Is a Duty 144

Conclusion 147
About the Author 149

Acknowledgements

I am grateful to God for the gift of salvation and the privilege to serve in His vineyard. Daily, I see His hand leading, navigating, and orchestrating events for His glory, in my life and in my ministry. Let all the glory be to Him alone.

I acknowledge the men and women used of God in various ways and at various times to bring me to where I am today.

Thank you, Pastor Tony Rapu, senior pastor of This Present House, Lagos. He has been our pastor from the very beginning of our journey, before this vision was even birthed many years ago, and he is still our pastor today.

To our spiritual dad, Dr Okey Onuzo; your prayers and counsel have greatly influenced and shaped this work.

To Pastor Olu Obanure, thank you for being attentive to the Spirit of God in believing and supporting us when we came to share this vision with you. There was no outward reason for you to have believed us, except by the Spirit of God.

To every member of the Joyforce, fantastic men and women who voluntarily chose to lay their hands on the plough; you are all God's blessing to me.

To all the members of the media team, used by God mightily to make this work possible; the Lord will surely reward your labour of love.

Finally, to my family: my wife and copastor Chineze; and my children, Uchechukwu and Tochukwu. You are God's gift, designed, packaged and delivered to me.

May the Lord continue His marvellous work in each and every one of us as He transforms His church into the desired bride of the Lamb.

God bless you!

And I thank Christ Jesus our Lord who has enabled me, because He counted me faithful, putting me into the ministry, although I was formerly a blasphemer, a persecutor, and an insolent man; but I obtained mercy because I did it ignorantly in unbelief. And the grace of our Lord was exceedingly abundant, with faith and love which are in Christ Jesus. (1 Timothy 1:12–14 NKJV)

Introduction

Our Lord Jesus said,

> Therefore do not worry, saying, 'What shall we eat?' or 'What shall we drink?' or 'What shall we wear?' For after all these things the Gentiles seek. For your heavenly Father knows that you need all these things. But seek first the kingdom of God and His righteousness, and all these things shall be added to you. (Matthew 6:31–33 NKJV)

If the word 'first' is removed from the verse of scripture above, it will sound alike but will never mean the same. 'First' means coming before all others in time or order, earliest, foremost in position, rank, or importance. The *Oxford Online Dictionary* has this to say about 'first':

- The ordinal number matching the number one in a series.
- The one coming, occurring, or ranking before or above all others.
- The beginning; the outset: from the first; at first.
(Oxford Online Dictionary, 2016)

If the scripture above is not properly understood, one may be tempted to think that our Lord Jesus is asking us not to seek after our welfare. What He said is to place God before the rest. It means that the other things are not excluded but come after the first. According to the dictionary, 'first' means *the one coming, occurring, or ranking before or above all others.*

The requirements for a good life are not condemned. Unlike the Gentiles, who place the other things first, He advised His followers to place seeking God and His kingdom as first, to be followed by the others.

The adversary for too long has deceived us. He was described as the most cunning of all creatures and was responsible for the tragedy that occurred at the garden of Eden. As always, his motive is to thwart our relationship with God our Father by bringing every manner of 'defensibly genuine' issues or needs to distract us or shift our focus; thereafter, he turns around to accuse us as undeserving of the mercy and goodness of God.

What I find interesting is the fact that over these generations, his strategy has hardly changed. He utilizes the same basic principles albeit in different packages. The primary tool of his trade is *deception*.

I urge you to prayerfully read through this book inspired by the Spirit of God with your Bible at hand. Let us see practical ways to enforce the victory Jesus won on our behalf and live victorious lives here on earth.

May the Lord quicken your spirit!

Part One

Give Him First Place

1

His Rightful Place

Creator without Need

God created the world for His pleasure, not out of need; He has no material need other than the salvation of mankind. He is all sufficient and is known as the self-existing God. The presence of God assures that every good thing is in full and abundant supply.

In the beginning, God created Eden and placed man in it: 'The Lord God planted a garden eastward in Eden, and there He put the man whom He had formed' (Genesis 2:8 NKJV). God sought to meet His pleasure by fellowshipping with man. In the cool of the day, God would come down to commune with Adam. The presence, curiosity, and creativity of Adam and his way of interacting with Creation gave God immense pleasure.

> Out of the ground the Lord God formed every beast of the field and every bird of the air, and brought them to Adam to see what he would call them. And whatever Adam called each living creature, that was its name. (Genesis 2:19 NKJV)

Creation of Need

On the other hand, man is a creation of need whose basis for sustained life is anchored on the supply of essentials, such as air, water, and food.

Only God is without need for by Him, through Him, and for Him do all things exist.

In this context, we can define a living thing as one that is in a state of need; a living thing is a 'needy thing'. To be living is to be needing; to be alive is to be in need. The only way to stop needing is to die. All living things have insatiable needs, and the satisfaction of one creates the need for another; that is just how God created His world.

His Love

If there was ever a contest as regards the most popular or best-known verse in the Bible, the prize would almost certainly go to John 3:16 (NKJV): 'For God so loved the world that He gave His only begotten Son, that whoever believes in Him should not perish but have everlasting life.' This scripture brings to life the divine plan for the redemption of mankind, God's beloved creation, after the tragedy and distortion brought about by sin and disobedience.

> For if by the one man's offense death reigned through the one, much more those who receive abundance of grace and of the gift of righteousness will reign in life through the One, Jesus Christ. Therefore, as through one man's offense judgment came to all men, resulting in condemnation, even so through one Man's righteous act the free gift came to all men, resulting in justification of life. For as by one man's disobedience many were made sinners, so also by one Man's obedience many will be made righteous. (Romans 5:17–19 NKJV)

The actions of God are always motivated by His love; indeed scripture states clearly that God is love and that anyone who claims to be of God but does not love is of the devil (1 John 4:7–8). This love motivated Him, as stated in John 3:16, to send His son, Jesus, to redeem us from the bondage of sin.

Unfortunately, embedded in the nature of man is a desire to pursue self-sufficiency, which breeds frustration. In part, this desire explains the catastrophe at the garden of Eden. The undoing of human beings is usually an attempt to operate outside their design, mandate, and capacity. The wise person is one who has come to accept that being in a 'God-needy' state is just the way God created him to be.

When we approach God in love and vulnerability, He relates to us with joy and eagerness. Indeed, satisfying our needs have always been pleasurable to Him. This means that our issues are nothing before God. As long as our needs are being channelled to the one who made us and is never surprised by our needs, they will be met.

Once our eyes become open to how great our God is and how deeply He loves us, the natural reaction should be to seek to know Him more. Our objective is simply to work towards developing greater appetite and capacity to love God more than we currently do.

In his letter to the Colossians, apostle Paul stated as follows:

> For this reason we also, since the day we heard it, do not cease to pray for you, and to ask that you may be filled with the knowledge of His will in all wisdom and spiritual understanding; that you may walk worthy of the Lord, fully pleasing Him, being fruitful in every good work and increasing in the knowledge of God. (Colossians 1:9–10 NKJV)

This scripture is a heartfelt prayer for us to walk in a wisdom that cannot be taught in schools—a wisdom that revealed to Moses those things that had taken place before he came on the scene and made it possible for him to write those first books of the Bible. This wisdom is unsearchable, immeasurable, and uncontainable in its scope and dimensions.

The principles stated in the Bible would appear abstract if there were no examples to bring them alive. This principle of the 'first' is no exception. A case in point is the prophet Elijah and the widow in 1 Kings 17:8, when God instructs the prophet to go for sustenance in the time of the famine.

The Bible states:

> Then the word of the Lord came to him, saying, "Arise, go to Zarephath, which belongs to Sidon, and

> dwell there. See, I have commanded a widow there to provide for you." So he arose and went to Zarephath. And when he came to the gate of the city, indeed a widow was there gathering stick. And he called to her and said, "Please bring me a little water in a cup, that I may drink." And as she was going to get it, he called to her and said, "Please bring me a morsel of bread in your hand." So she said, "As the Lord your God lives, I do not have bread, only a handful of flour in a bin, and a little oil in a jar; and see, I am gathering a couple of sticks that I may go in and prepare it for myself and my son, that we may eat it, and die." And Elijah said to her, "Do not fear; go and do as you have said, but make me a small cake from it first, and bring it to me; and afterward make some for yourself and your son. (1 Kings 17:8–13 NKJV)

The miracle that followed this encounter is possible in each and every one of our lives. The prophet promised her that the flour and oil would never run out if she complied with his request. The test was simple but distressing since feeding the prophet in this circumstance was akin to her dying. Indeed, all she had was a little flour and a little oil to bake a cake.

Many Christians compromise because they are afraid of something that may happen as a consequence of their obedience to God. This woman was able to confront and conquer the fear of imminent death from hunger hanging over her if she fed the prophet. Death was already by her, but obeying the prophet opened up a new dimension to which she connected by faith.

Sometimes we feel that God should trust us since He is almighty, but that's not how things work. How easy is it to get your bank to stamp and acknowledge a certificate of deposit before you part with your money? The right process is to hand over your cash or instrument; in exchange, you will receive a piece of paper acknowledging that you made a deposit or whatever transaction. That commercial bank will be treated the same way they treat their customers if it has any reason to transact with the Central Bank of Nigeria (CBN). The reason for this is simple: the lesser is obligated to exercise trust and confidence in the greater.

When God says, 'Seek Me first,' it is because every other thing is designed to take its bearing or position from what is first. In fact, whatever you place first determines what comes after it. Everything depends on it. Many of us distort this order; we take the things that should come after and place them ahead of what should be first. This distortion certainly ensures that nothing glorious and lasting comes out of our efforts.

Once you become a Christian, one thing becomes needful and critical: giving God first place. This becomes an ongoing daily battle for the rest of your life. The dynamics may change in each case or situation, but the fundamentals will remain the same. Neglecting this singular fact has caused many frustrations and disappointments.

This principle of the first made the critical difference between Cain and Abel. Cain brought something from his produce which was not the first, while Abel brought the firstborn of his animals. One was the first, the other was at random, and the outcomes speak for themselves.

In every area of your marriage, business, and life, it is vital to remember that you are, first and foremost, a Christian. This reality dominates every other one and must come first. No matter what your circumstances are, the most important factor is to remember what is first. Settling this question removes every other option and things that jostle to occupy this prime position.

Some people make adjustments and place God last in their scheme of things, especially when confronted with a dire situation. One can almost imagine them saying, 'If God can wait until I solve this problem, I will serve Him.' How outright unwise and impudent is such a stance!

Look back at the prayer in Colossians:

> For this reason we also, since the day we heard it, do not cease to pray for you, and to ask that you may be filled with the knowledge of His will in all wisdom and spiritual understanding. (Colossians 1:9 NKJV)

It is evident that right understanding is needful in our walk with God. Giving Him preference over and above every other thing is what determines a glorious outcome.

This principle permeates every other aspect of our lives. If serving

God were the reason you work hard for a financial breakthrough, then it would not matter so much to you if that breakthrough failed to materialize. Depression comes because the motivation and intent of our hearts is very far from honouring God above all else. We get frustrated because our focus is to satisfy those things that ought to be additions.

Adam and Eve failed their test in the garden of Eden. God had created every tree that was pleasant to the sight, good for food and the tree of life was also in the midst of the garden. But God commanded them to eat of every tree except the tree of knowledge of good and evil (Genesis 2:9–16). Then the serpent, which was clever, cleverer than any other animal God had made spoke to the woman, saying,

> Do I understand that God told you not to eat from any tree in the garden? (Genesis 3:1 MSG).

This simple question from the serpent to Eve was the catalyst that led to the fall of Adam and Eve; eventually, they were driven from the garden, ending their fellowship with God.

The serpent deceived Eve by twisting what God said, which altered the meaning entirely. If only Eve had asked God for clarity, assuming she was confused by His instructions. Eventually, she doubted the faithfulness of God and focussed more on what He asked her not to do rather than completely obeying Him. That deception continues even today, where believers judge God wrongly in their circumstances.

The less desires you have, the less sin you can commit. Where there is no need, there can be no sin. So the less desires we have, the less need we have. Need itself is not a problem; rather, a need channelled to the wrong source is a problem. The consequence of sin is that it cuts off fellowship with God, creating a void and making us avoid God.

Living contrary to God's commands in any way whatsoever is the major pitfall of the children of God. Sin is simply mismatching needs and solutions. God has provided a fulfilment to every human need. If you find your life looking depressing, and not as God promised, seek Him more. The rightful fulfilment to every need and expectation reside in Him.

2

100% SAVED!

Contrary to the lie that the adversary will have us believe; God is indeed desirous and committed to the total welfare of His Children. The Bible states as follows,

> Beloved, I pray that you may prosper in all things and be in health, just as your soul prospers. (3 John 2 NKJV)

God's desire is that His children are prosperous in all aspects of life. For Him, prosperity and righteousness are inseparable. Salvation cannot be quantified. Indeed, it cannot be measured. However, the extent to which one exhibits the character consistent with salvation in daily choices can be measured. God's plan for the salvation of mankind is comprehensive, but it requires the acceptance and subsequent cooperation of each individual to become complete.

In the text before us, *'Prosper* (in all things) *and be in health as your soul prospers'* is an action word from the Author of Life to His creation—a license for the believer's basic living on earth. Nothing less! God desires that you flourish, do well, succeed, make money, thrive in this life, and be fit, strong, and healthy—but not to the detriment of your soul.

The promise of God to Abraham regarding his descendants in Egypt had a period of four hundred years. The Jews were oblivious of this agreement and were more mindful of their material possessions and the splendid onions, garlic, and cucumbers they were enjoying in Egypt. They had seen many years of 'enjoyment', eating and being merry without thinking of the promises of God to Abraham. The problem with this kind of existence is that one is oblivious of the dangers that lie ahead.

It was a rude shock for them when a Pharaoh who did not know Joseph came on the throne and began to afflict and oppress them.

> Now there arose a new king over Egypt, who did not know Joseph. (Exodus 1:8 NKJV)

It was at this time that they began to cry to God, remembering His promise to Abraham. Things went from bad to worse soon after the return of Moses with the message of liberation and deliverance from the God of their fathers, who appeared to him on Mount Sinai. It got so bad that Moses was thought to be more of a curse to them than a blessing.

What they failed to realize was that God had great plans for them, not just in that present situation but also in the future. Moses had been sent for their total deliverance, although in the immediate, the deliverance process was causing them terrible hardship.

In the course of striving to bring them out of Egypt following the devastating impact of the plagues—turning water into blood, frogs, lice, and flies—Pharaoh offered to allow them worship in the land but without leaving Egypt.

He said to Moses in Exodus 8:25 (NIV), 'Go, sacrifice to your God here in the land.'

The enemy never wants to let the believers out of his vicinity; he wants you to remain in his territory though you are now in Christ. He wants to have your health, finances, and children while you are serving God. It is heartbreaking to see him succeed with these schemes. The plan of God is for the total redemption of man; nothing should be left behind in the camp of the enemy.

The Christian walk with God should never be based on feelings and emotions alone. We are to engage the Word of God as it comes to us intent on obedience. If we fail to do so, our opportunities for change, prosperity, and advancement may be lost or wasted.

Moses, refusing to succumb to Pharaoh's offer, stuck with what God had said, and in Exodus 10:26 (NKJV), he said,

Our livestock also shall go with us; not a hoof shall be left behind. For we must take some of them to serve the Lord our God, and even we do not know with what we must serve the Lord until we arrive there.

Refuse to accept anything less than the best of all that God has given you in Christ. Salvation can be 100 per cent experientially even as it is spiritually. As scripture puts it,

> His divine power has given to us all things that pertain to life and godliness, through the knowledge of Him who called us. (2 Peter 1:3 NKJV)

Moses said, 'And even we do not know with what we must serve the Lord until we arrive there.'

This scripture highlights for us the importance of the total freedom of the believer. Every aspect of our lives and all that pertains to us must be free and sanctified, ready for His use. Everything must be used for His glory; nothing should be tainted by the corruption of our adversary. Righteousness and holiness are non-negotiable once we have come to the conviction of an eternal walk with God.

3

FOLLOW THE CLOUD

As we continue our reflection on how God took a people from a nation to a destination He had promised their forefathers, let us take a moment to ponder over the dynamics of this journey. One wonders if they were even aware of this promise at that point in their national life. But the faithfulness of the One that promised, the One who swore by Himself and delivered them from the land of bondage.

We know the range of events that took place on this journey and the challenges that were orchestrated by the mixed multitude. Among the vital instructions that God gave them, the only guarantee to getting to their destination was by following the cloud of His presence.

The Bible says in Numbers 9:17–19 (NKJV),

> Whenever the cloud was taken up from above the tabernacle, after that the children of Israel would journey; and in the place where the cloud settled, there the children of Israel would pitch their tents. At the command of the Lord the children of Israel would journey, and at the command of the Lord they would camp; as long as the cloud stayed above the tabernacle they remained encamped. Even when the cloud continued long, many days above the tabernacle, the children of Israel kept the charge of the Lord and did not journey.

Verses 20–22 say,

> So it was, when the cloud remained only from evening until morning: when the cloud was taken up in the morning, then they would journey; whether by day or by night, whenever the cloud was taken up, they would journey and according to the command of the Lord they would journey.

Do you see something here? Whether it was day or night didn't matter; as long as the cloud lifted over the tabernacle, they followed it. They simply followed whichever direction the cloud went and camped wherever it stopped. That is the life of the believer. The believer follows the Holy Spirit.

Whether it was two days, a month, or a year that the cloud remained above the tabernacle, the children of Israel would remain encamped and not journey; but when it was taken up, they would journey.

God will usually give you something or someone that can serve as a guide. If you have learned about discipleship, you know that a disciple is the one that follows. To follow simply means to go after or to come after something or somebody.

In this case, as referenced in scripture, the pillar of cloud was leading, but it was their responsibility to follow. It served to provide shade over them in the hot desert sun and to give them light when it was dark.

Today, the cloud for us to follow as believers is the Holy Spirit. As believers, we are to follow the leading of the Holy Spirit.

> *For as many as are led by the Spirit of God, these are sons of God.* (Romans 8:14 NKJV)

God desires that all His children can hear him clearly, our Lord Jesus said:

> But you do not believe, because you are not of My sheep, as I said to you. My sheep hear My voice, and I know them, and they follow Me. (John 10:27–28 NKJV)

You must be mindful of what you are following because it will ultimately determine where you go and where you end up. Many believers have followed the wrong things, seeking their own glory through personal accomplishments. They forget that those accomplishments vanish in a short time.

The approval of God over a man is not measured by whether he has a credit balance or debit balance. That a business transaction will render immense profit does not necessarily mean it is from God. If we were to scripturally analyse or scrutinize the process that resulted in some testimonies that people share in Church and fellowships, it would be obvious that some of them would have brought disappointment to the cloud of witnesses in heaven.

The heroes of faith obtained good testimony not material possessions. Let nobody deceive you; let nobody make you feel unfortunate on the premise that you have little faith since you have little material possessions. Great faith is shown by good testimony; great faith is not evidenced by great acquisition. A great acquisition may be evidence of greed.

Jesus taught us that the life of a man does not consist in the abundance of things that he possesses:

> And He said to them, "Take heed and beware of covetousness, for one's life does not consist in the abundance of the things he possesses." (Luke 12:15 NKJV)

This was a warning rather than an advice; it is wise to take heed indeed.

How to Follow the Cloud

> Moses said to God, "Look, you tell me, 'Lead this people,' but you don't let me know whom you're going to send with me. You tell me, 'I know you well and you are special to me.' If I am so special to you, let me in on your plans. That way, I will continue being special to you. Don't forget, this is your people, your responsibility." God said, "My presence will go with you. I'll see the journey to the end." Moses said, "If your presence doesn't take the lead here, call this trip off right now. How else will it be known that you're with me in this, with me and your people? Are

you traveling with us or not? How else will we know that we're special, I and your people, among all other people on this planet Earth?" (Exodus 33:12–16 MSG)

Verses 16–17 say,

> For how then will it be known that Your people and I have found grace in Your sight, except You go with us? So we shall be separate, Your people and I, from all the people who are upon the face of the earth." So the Lord said to Moses, "I will also do this thing that you have spoken; for you have found grace in My sight, and I know you by name. (NKJV)

You Need to Know, so Ask

This is a prayer, a call to God. Moses was having a conversation with Him. He had brought the people of Israel out and was informing Moses of His plans, Moses said to Him, 'Well I have heard all these things that You are saying, but I want to understand how it is going to be. How will I know that we are continuing in this?'

Remember—Moses as a child was a peculiar one; he was different from the rest of his generation. He was peculiarly preserved by God and had discerned that he was a deliverer. At the age of 40, he rose up to fulfil the ministry he was convinced that God committed in his hands. You know what happened, how disastrous that attempt was; he ended up murdering a man and being accused by the same people that he had come to deliver (Exodus 2:11–15), so Moses was here being very circumspect.

> 'Lord let's take our time let's understand how this will work.'

That is why he said to God, 'It is Your responsibility. I didn't decide to do this. I gave You all my reasons: I am a stammerer. You know I am a fugitive, and upon all of that, You still brought me in, so let me understand how this is going to work.'

And for us today, for the child of God in our generation, it's also applicable. As we engage with the word of God, we must set out time to meditate on it and ask Him how to proceed.

The Bible says, 'How can a young man cleanse his ways?' (Psalm 119:9 NKJV).

For you to make it in this Christian walk, you must ask God, 'How do we do this? How is it going to work? How will I pay my bills? How will I survive? How will I triumph? How can I make my marriage work? How can I stay clean in a place like Nigeria? How am I going to make it?'

That was what formed the basis of this discussion. And it applies to you and me because things can get so confusing in the world we live in today. You need something more definite or distinct beyond your emotions.

We need to be able to tell God, 'I don't want to miss it, I don't want anybody to deceive me, and I don't want to deceive anybody. I want to make sure that what I am saying, what I am doing, what I am hearing; who I am following and the path I am on, is the right one for me.

We live in a world where examinations, tests, and proof have become very necessary because things are not the way they appear anymore. In today's world, if somebody sends you his photograph in advance and says, 'You meet me at the airport,' you have to ask him to carry his name as well because photo identifications are no longer sufficient. This is because, depending on how you want to appear, you can use computer software tools to stretch a plump person to be very slim, or alter anybody's features into something more appealing, so that when you compare some person's images to the actual person, you will hardly believe your eyes.

Years before now, if somebody was in a faraway city and sent you a letter, you would see the stamp of the post office of that city on the envelope. All that is different in this electronic world we live in today. When communicating electronically, you can be in the same physical location with someone, and that person may claim to be somewhere else.

We must ask God to guide us through the tests necessary to be confident and assured in Him and no other. This was the core of this conversation Moses had with God. The Lord said to him, 'I will bring My presence with you.'

It is important to note that God didn't say to Moses, 'Miracles will always happen where you are,' because one of the things we are sure of in these last days is that the devil will work many lying wonders. The devil knows the word of God and maximizes every opportunity that is given to him. However, permission is given to him in the last days to do what? *Work miracles and lying wonders.* Therefore, simply that a miracle has been performed does not mean that God is there.

In this discussion, Moses asked God to give him a 'litmus test'. If you remember your basic science, a litmus test is one whose outcome is determined by only one variable, not two. That is, if I see this colour, then I am sure it is X and not Y. The litmus test when carried out says a solution is either acid or alkaline; it can only prove one, not two.

If you are single, for example, let me describe a valid litmus test. If you are born again and the person you are in courtship with does not honour the word of God, just run. Nobody can love you more than he or she loves your God. No man can love you more than he loves Jesus. If the man doesn't love Jesus and he is buying you roses and throwing petals on the floor while you walk, run. That's a litmus test, one sign that tells everything.

In this conversation, Moses told the Lord to give him a litmus test, and the Lord said, 'It is My presence.' Notice that He didn't tell him that the people will always agree with him. That's not what the Lord promised him because several times they even wanted to stone him. He didn't promise him that he will never have challenges; in fact, he had challenges continually.

There Is a Process

The Bible says that the gifts and calling of God are without repentance. Sometimes I wish it weren't so, since people have gone to hell with gifts and callings. People have lost destinies functioning in gifts; I wish God would withdraw every gift the moment a person stepped out of line.

When God wants to really bless you, He is concerned about everything including the testimony along the way. The devil does not bother about the process, as his objective is always sinister. He will utilize whatever is ungodly such as kidnapping, oil bunkering, and any other evil means available. When God chooses to work with you, even the minutest things will be taken into consideration to ensure a perfect work is achieved.

In the account in Judges 9:5, after the death of Gideon, Abimelech his son rose up in one day and killed his seventy brothers and became king; the devil doesn't consider the process.

When God anointed David King of Israel, consider how long it took to bring him to the throne from the time that Samuel first anointed him king in the stead of Saul:

> So he sent and brought him in. Now he was ruddy, with bright eyes, and good-looking. And the LORD said, "Arise, anoint him; for this is the one!" Then Samuel took the horn of oil and anointed him in the midst of his brothers; and the Spirit of the LORD came upon David from that day forward. So Samuel arose and went to Ramah. (1 Samuel 16:12 NKJV)

God had to make sure that Saul was eased out of the kingship without David offending. Many years later, the elders of Israel came and submitted to David.

> Therefore all the elders of Israel came to the king at Hebron, and King David made a covenant with them at Hebron before the LORD. And they anointed David king over Israel. David was thirty years old when he began to reign, and he reigned forty years. In Hebron he reigned over Judah seven years and six months, and in Jerusalem he reigned thirty-three years over all Israel and Judah. (2 Samuel 5:3–5 NKJV)

If you are wondering, 'Why is my business not expanding and increasing rapidly?' it is likely that God is the One at work, taking you through a process of growth. His work goes through the essential process to bring about an unquestionable outcome.

It Was Not Convenient

When the nation of Israel followed the cloud, can I tell you what happened? Remember that God sent them manna daily. Sometimes, I imagine the manna could have dropped and as they are about to gather it, the cloud will lift and you see mothers calling, 'Jimmy, Tony, let's go.'

Tony says, 'I haven't eaten.'

She says, 'See the cloud? Let's go.'

The man that is led by the Spirit will not move by convenience but by the Spirit of God. It is impossible to tell someone's standing with God simply by the events of their lives on this side of eternity. That your business seems to be experiencing a lull or you are facing a challenge in your health does not mean that God is no longer happy with you; that is the lie of the devil. Have you heard of the refiner's fire? Did Jesus not teach us what He does when a tree bears fruit? He prunes it that it may bear much fruit.

The woman that God used to feed the prophet had just one meal but abundance afterwards (1 Kings 17:8–16). Let me ask you, if that woman didn't feed the prophet, what would have happened to her? I hope you know that she would have died? Thank God she obeyed the word of the prophet.

You can't live your Christian life like a toy car that reverses the moment it hits an obstacle. It's not everywhere you hit an obstacle that there is a roadblock. Sometimes there is a goldmine; there may be treasure and greatness. The breakthrough you believe God for may be packaged as trouble.

Your Testimony Is God's Responsibility

Do you know that if you are born again, your testimony is God's responsibility? Let me take you back to the scripture referenced earlier in this chapter.

> If I am so special to you, let me in on your plans. That way, I will continue being special to you. Don't forget, this is your people, your responsibility. (Exodus 33:13 MSG)

How would you feel if your employees abandoned the jobs for which you paid them in order to run around to raise money to fuel their cars?

What would you say to them? They are supposed to give you their services in exchange for their salary and upkeep.

The child of God is God's responsibility. Although Moses spoke concerning the nation of Israel, you can apply this to your personal life. From the moment you surrendered your life to Jesus, He became your Lord and He became your Saviour. This means your well-being and welfare became His responsibility.

This explains why the third line in our Lord's Prayer says, 'Hallowed be Your name.'

It is an amazing prayer because for the name of your God to be hallowed, you can be used. When we say, 'Hallowed be Your name,' we are asking that the King be exalted, and when the King is exalted, His subjects are automatically exalted.

As earlier stated, the entire journey of the Israelites was under the direction and cover of the pillar of cloud, which was also the source of light when it became dark. It shielded them from the harsh sun of the desert and provided illumination during the night. In fact, when the army of Pharaoh was pursuing the people of God, the Bible records as follows:

> And the Angel of God, who went before the camp of Israel, moved and went behind them; and the pillar of cloud went from before them and stood behind them. So it came between the camp of the Egyptians and the camp of Israel. Thus it was a cloud and darkness to the one, and it gave light by night to the other, so that the one did not come near the other all that night. (Exodus 14:19–20 NKJV)

The presence of the Holy Spirit is the best gift that Jesus bestowed on every believer. The Spirit of God is the believer's assurance of everlasting victory over sin and death. He is our joy, peace, courage, as well as our confidence in battle.

4

CHANGE YOUR DIET

One of the most viable lifestyle business sectors in the world today is diet and fitness. Daily, we are bombarded with various propositions with promises of expected results from dietary programs and regimens.

Everyone desires good health and longevity, and we consequently make necessary adjustments in our lifestyle. This includes efforts in terms of food choices that will ensure fitness in appearance and general well-being.

However, it is essential to change your diet in accordance with your desired objective. The majority of people who go on a diet desire wish to reduce body weight. Some are placed on a diet so they can gain weight (likely following convalescence from illness). So, depending on the desired outcome, various dietary programs can be initiated and followed.

The children of Israel had enjoyed a dietary regimen for many generations during their stay in Egypt. They had become used to the cucumbers, onions, garlic, and the 'fish bought without money' of Egypt. When it was time to change their diet based on a higher calling, it was a challenge for them. They kept looking back and yearning for the garlic and onions of Egypt instead of looking forward to the milk and honey of the Promised Land.

> Now the mixed multitude who were among them yielded to intense craving; so the children of Israel also wept again and said: "Who will give us meat to eat? We remember the fish which we ate freely in Egypt, the cucumbers, the melons, the leeks, the onions, and the garlic; but now our whole being is dried up; there is nothing at all except this manna before our eyes! (Numbers 11:5–6 NKJV)

It was necessarily symbolic for them to develop an appetite different from what they had been used to in Egypt. As I stated earlier, the dietary program is usually designed with an objective in mind. This is the reason I am introducing to you another kind of diet, capable of sustaining you as a believer against the wiles of the evil. It is the diet of the Word of God.

We all know that the sole aim of our Arch-enemy, the devil, *is to steal, kill and destroy the believer* (John 10:10). It is quite easy to picture the thieves or armed robbers stealing from us our precious property whenever a thief is mentioned. We guard ourselves against them by securing our homes, cars, and other valuables. However, we do nothing to guard ourselves against the main thief, the devil, who steals from us without our knowledge because his approach to theft is not conventional.

This thief comes to steal our righteousness, peace, and joy because he understands that this is the kingdom of God. Remember how Adam and Eve lost their glory at the garden of Eden. After being tempted by the devil, they went into hiding from the presence of God. So by their act of disobedience, the devil stole their glory without them truly realizing it.

The glory was given to them as a covering, but he took it from them. He left them completely naked and desires to do the same thing to us. When a person is left in darkness, after a while, he may become accustomed to the darkness and even find light abhorrent.

The same way when the enemy comes, he works hard to steal our righteousness, which is our covering. He does this by tempting us to compromise, disobey, and sin against God. Every temptation that comes to you as a believer is intended to take away your glory, so get dressed, and do not allow the devil to steal your glory. Neither allow him to steal your joy and peace.

The greatest heist the devil has carried out on the Church is the lie that it is okay and understandable not to completely obey the word of God. We get excited on hearing a powerful message preached but forget to do what the word says. What we hear alone brings no benefit except when we practice and exercise ourselves in them.

> This Book of the Law shall not depart from your mouth, but you shall meditate in it day and night, that you may observe to do according to all that is written in

it. For then you will make your way prosperous, and then you will have good success. (Joshua 1:8 NKJV)

The only condition given to Joshua was to observe to do, that is to obey. He received encouragement to be strong and courageous so that he would find the strength to obey (Joshua 1:7).

In Luke 8:5, Jesus used the parable of the sower for clearer understanding and for emphasis on the value of taking the word of God seriously, so he cried, 'He that has an ear let him hear.' In other words, take note:

A sower went out to sow his seed. And as he sowed, some fell by the wayside; and it was trampled down, and the birds of the air devoured it. Some fell on rock; and as soon as it sprang up, it withered away because it lacked moisture. And some fell among thorns, and the thorns sprang up with it and choked it. But others fell on good ground, sprang up, and yielded a crop a hundredfold." When He had said these things He cried, "He who has ears to hear, let him hear!" (Luke 8:12 NKJV)

Note that the devil did not stop them from hearing; in fact, he leaves it ringing in their ears since there is no benefit in their hearts. The evidence that you have truly heard the word of God is when you decide to obey; the fruit of obedience will then be evidence that the word was not stolen from your heart.

We must take the word of God and dwell on it constantly because only then can we truly learn to place it above everything else.

If you truly want to make advancement, then make adjustments in your life for the word 'for faith comes by hearing and hearing the word of God' (Romans 10:17 NKJV). The only thing that can change your mind is your spiritual diet.

When the devil came to tempt Jesus after He had fasted for forty days and nights, he was not just testing his physical appetite. He was bringing a doctrine that Jesus was careful to rebuke. He was subtly saying, 'You can work from your external to your internal' (you can let what is outside sustain what is inside). But Jesus hushed him, saying,

> It is written, man shall not live by bread alone but by every word that proceeds from the mouth of God. (Luke 4:4 NKJV).

This means that as surely as my physical life is sustained by the food I eat, the same way my spiritual life is also sustained and determined by the word of God I hear, understand and practice. I must, therefore, be conscious not to be malnourished spiritually.

Ultimately, Jesus was saying, 'Although I can go without physical food for a period [forty days], I cannot survive without the word of God.'

The Bible says,

> The spirit of a man will sustain him in sickness,
> But who can bear a broken spirit? (Proverbs 18:14 NKJV)

Many times, people have survived life-threatening sicknesses because they were strong on the inside. As the Bible puts it,

> Even though our outward man is perishing, yet the inward man is being renewed day by day. (2 Corinthians 4:16 NKJV)

Friends, the Spirit of God in us is more essential and critical to the outcome of our lives than any other factor. The heathen kings testified of Daniel 'in whom is the Spirit of the Holy God'. Therefore, popularity or environment does not determine a man's destiny in life. There is a diet that can change your level; it is the diet of the word of God.

> For the word of God is living and powerful, and sharper than any two-edged sword, piercing even to the division of soul and spirit, and of joints and marrow, and is a discerner of the thoughts and intents of the heart. (Hebrews 4:12 NKJV)

Change your diet to that of the word of God, and make it your necessary occupation. It will serve you at all times and in all circumstances.

5

EAT OF THE TREE OF LIFE

The garden of Eden was a beautiful place prepared by God. It was His design to give man a blissful life as conveyed by Genesis 2:9 (NKJV):

> And out of the ground the Lord God made every tree grow that is pleasant to the sight and good for food. The tree of life was also in the midst of the garden, and the tree of the knowledge of good and evil.

God placed Adam in the garden of Eden and said to him,

> Of all the trees in the Garden you may freely eat but of the tree of the knowledge of good and evil thou shalt not eat for in the day you eat of it, you shall surely die. (Genesis 2:16–17 ESV)

God's instruction was clear: 'Eat of every tree in the garden except of the tree of the knowledge of good and evil.' Therefore, by inference, we can say that Adam was permitted to eat from the tree of life but chose not to eat. He ate instead from every other tree in the garden and subsequently the forbidden tree of the knowledge of good and evil. From that moment, the problems of the world began (Romans 5:12).

The problems that exist today, regardless of how they manifest, were brought about by a deficiency of the tree of life. Jesus, speaking to the paralytic in Luke 5:20, said to him, 'Your sins are forgiven,' implying that the root of every sickness is sin.

Sin is not the many 'names' we call them, such as fornication, backbiting, gossiping, stealing, etc.; all these are symptoms. Sin is like a virus that enters into a system and disrupts its normal functions; it manifests various symptoms to make known its presence.

God said to Cain,

> If you do well, shall you not be accepted? And if you do not well, sin lies at the door. It desires to subdue you but you must rule over it. (Genesis 4:7 NKJV)

Therefore, sin is not first of all an action; it is a spirit. Jesus wanted to teach the people present in the gathering that there is a spirit behind sickness, pain, sorrow, suffering, wickedness, murders, mischief, and every other evil in the world, and it is called sin.

When God sent man out of the garden of Eden, he placed cherubs in the garden to guard the way to the tree of life to prevent man from gaining access to it. He gave us Jesus Christ the tree of life. God planted the tree of life in the midst of the earth with the intent of purging the world of all impurities, and the life of Jesus exemplifies this, as stated in Revelation 22:2 (NKJV):

> In the middle of its street, and on either side of the river, was the tree of life, which bore twelve fruits, each tree yielding its fruit every month. The leaves of the tree were for the healing of the nations.

Adam made the mistake of eating from every other tree in the garden of Eden except the tree of life, which is the same thing the religions of the world achieve; giving from every other tree except the one extremely fundamental to your well-being.

Our Lord Jesus said to the Jews,

> You search the Scriptures because you think that in them you have eternal life; and they testify about me, yet you refuse to come to me that you may have life. (John 5:39–40 ESV)

There is a way out of the many troubles we see, a way to live life victoriously. Jesus lived a victorious life. He walked through the crowd that wanted to stone him untouched and escaped many dangers unharmed. The mountain of accusations against him could not be justified because he lived according to the will of God. When you live according to the precepts of God, you will have victory.

It is true that Adam made wrong choices that spiralled into the current tribulations in the world, but the question is 'What choices are you making?' Are you going for the things on the surface, things that gratify the flesh, or are you taking a decision to eat from the tree of life?

> So when the woman saw that the tree was good for food, that it was pleasant to the eyes, and a tree desirable to make one wise, she took of its fruit and ate. She also gave to her husband with her, and he ate. (Genesis 3:6 NKJV)

If someone read your story in years to come, what would be his or her conclusion? What kind of choices are you making in your daily activities? Like Jesus, our example, can your ultimate motivation be like His own?

> Jesus said to them, "My food is to do the will of Him who sent Me, and to finish His work." (John 4:34 NKJV)

The things that you believe God for are temporary, do not let them burden or influence your choices. It is God's will that you have every good thing that you desire, but He knows what is best for you and when you are ready to receive them. Why should a Christian become depressed because of temporary things when God has given him the Holy Spirit as guide?

In Matthew 7:11 and Luke 11:13, the terms 'Holy Spirit' and 'Good thing' were used interchangeably. This means that the 'Holy Spirit' and 'Good thing' are the same.

> If you then, being evil, know how to give good gifts to your children, how much more will your Father who is in heaven give good things to those who ask Him! (Matthew 7:11 NKJV)

> If you then, being evil, know how to give good gifts to your children, how much more will your heavenly Father give the Holy Spirit to those who ask Him! (Luke 11:13 NKJV)

You cry to God for 'things' but fail to understand that He has given you the Holy Spirit, who will guide you into all truth.

You may find yourself in a situation where it seems everything is against you but the Holy Spirit floods your heart with joy. The Bible says the kingdom of God is not in eating and drinking but righteousness, peace, and joy in the Holy Ghost (Romans 14:17).

There are people who have held on to 'things' and lost their ability to hear from God. Some are involved in ventures that are not necessarily bad, but the Holy Spirit has instructed them to discontinue; yet they insist on doing those things to the detriment of their peace and fellowship with God. The allures of this world have not allowed many to come to the cross and experience the freedom from the bonds of the adversary.

The scripture says if any man be in Christ, He is a new creature. Old things have passed away. Behold all things have become new (2 Corinthians 5:17).

When Christ comes into your life, the life that He brings should permeate every dimension of your living.

Jesus is the tree of life; do not neglect to eat of this tree. As the Lord Himself said, 'Most assuredly, I say to you, unless you eat the flesh of the Son of Man and drink His blood, you have no life in you' (John 6:53 NKJV).

Part Two

A Certain Future and an Expected End

6

IF GOD BE FOR US

> If God is for us, who can be against us? (Romans 8:31 NKJV)

In part one, we considered the dynamics of events that culminated in the fall of man and the scenario that unfolded as a consequence. We also reviewed the journey of the Israelites out of Egypt and how it relates to our lives today as believers. We concluded that the only sure way to victory on this journey is to give God first place in our lives. No matter how foolish it may sound to the world, it is the only path to eternal victory.

From the creation story, it is clear that everything was brought to existence by the spoken Word of God: earth, sea, sky, light, birds, fishes, animals, day, night. We also understand that there is a world that is not visible to the physical senses but is nonetheless active and superior to the physical world.

The fact that we encounter difficulties and challenges along the way should not make us question the sovereignty of God over His creation. Having this settled in our hearts early on, our journey of faith secures us like the anchor secures the ship.

No matter the conflict and dynamics of power arrayed against you, just one thing is needful: ensure you are on the same side with God. The side that God is on will always win.

> What then shall we say to these things? If God is for us, who can be against us? (Romans 8:31 NKJV)

The scripture above does not mean that conflicts will not arise if you are on God's side; rather, it means that the conflicts and controversies will fail and come to nothing. It means that once God is with you, it is entirely okay to ignore every other player on scene because the outcome is known and the matter concluded.

Is God with Me?

This is a critical question that every believer must find time to reflect on as we go about our activities. It enables us to sincerely and truthfully review our motivations and objectives, at the critical and challenging points of our existence. To answer this question is simple; where are you heading and who sent you there? If you are with Him, then he is with you.

Azariah the prophet said to King Asa,

> Hear me, Asa, and all Judah and Benjamin. The LORD is with you while you are with Him. If you seek Him, He will be found by you; but if you forsake Him, He will forsake you. (2 Chronicles 15:2 NKJV)

That I had a major breakthrough in business and family, including promotions and elevations at my secular job, does not guarantee that God is with me. Neither does the fact I suffered loss mean that God is not with me. The Church is culpable for projecting the mindset that if God is with you, temporary setbacks are not allowed. We must remember that it is only after the race that the winner is determined.

Direction here means where you are heading—towards the will of God, righteousness, peace, and joy in the Holy Ghost or in the opposite direction, away from God.

A Tale of Two Men

> Can two walk together except they be agreed? (Amos 3:3 NKJV)

Let us examine two instances of similar challenging situations that confronted two men at different times, generations, and locations. Looking at the stories of Jonah the prophet and apostle Paul, both were at different times in peril as passengers on ships threatening to capsize.

Jonah was heading in a direction contrary to the will and plan of God; He was running away to Tarshish when God sent him to Nineveh.

> Now the word of the LORD came to Jonah the son of Amittai, saying, "Arise, go to Nineveh, that great city, and cry out against it; for their wickedness has come up before Me." But Jonah arose to flee to Tarshish from the presence of the LORD. He went down to Joppa, and found a ship going to Tarshish; so he paid the fare, and went down into it, to go with them to Tarshish from the presence of the LORD. (Jonah 1:1–3 NKJV)

When the ship began to sink due to a severe contrary wind, he owned up to being at the centre of that divinely orchestrated elemental visitation. He was consequently thrown into the sea, and the Lord instructed a big fish to transport him to the shore. It was not just that he was thrown into the sea; he spent three unpleasant nights in the gut of the fish. God sent him to Nineveh that was close to where he was, but he chose to head to Tarshish, five times the distance to Nineveh from Joppa.

So, in Jonah's case, we see that the reason for his travails on the journey was disobedience, and his defiance even endangered his cotravellers; whereas for Paul, it was the refusal of the captain of the ship to heed his advice.

The map above provides us with clearer understanding of Jonah's folly and how many believers act even today.

On the other hand, Paul was on another voyage going in the direction that the Lord determined for him when he encountered the storm.

> But the following night the Lord stood by him and said, "Be of good cheer, Paul; for as you have testified for Me in Jerusalem, so you must also bear witness at Rome." (Acts 23:11 NKJV)

This was the purpose and direction of apostle Paul's journey when he encountered the adverse conditions with fellow prisoners and guards. He was on a journey that the Lord had commissioned and for a purpose already determined. So, in the time of turbulence, the angel of the Lord came to him as he recorded,

> But after long abstinence from food, then Paul stood in the midst of them and said, "Men, you should have listened to me, and not have sailed from Crete and incurred this disaster and loss. And now I urge you to take heart, for there will be no loss of life among you, but only of the ship. For there stood by me this night an angel of the God to whom I belong and whom I serve, saying, 'Do not be afraid, Paul; you must be brought before Caesar; and indeed God has granted you all those who sail with you." (Acts 27:21–24 NKJV)

He showed great courage and confidence because the angel of the Lord had appeared to him, reassuring him of his safety as well as the safety of his companions; he encouraged his fellow travellers to *take heart*.

Friends, no matter how fast you travel in the wrong direction, if you head away from God's will, your journey will be futile.

So we see that both men encountered situations that have to do with the sea and ships, their experience in the tribulation were completely different. How beautiful it is to be on the Lord's side.

Paul was heading in the direction God had determined, while Jonah sent himself to Tarshish away from God. Even in the remaining travails Paul encountered on this journey, the presence and power of God remained manifest.

Many believers will usually ask, 'If God is for me, why am I encountering these challenges?' God never promised us there would be no battles; rather, He promised that, at the end of the day, victory would be ours if we stay on His side. Did the shipwreck, the bite of the viper, and imprisonment mean that God was not with Paul? Indeed, there is no counsel or uprising against one who is on the Lord's side that would be considered successful at the end of the day.

Our battle is actually one-sided, ensuring that we are on the same side with God. The most important check for any Christian is to affirm continually that He is aligned to truth, honesty, and righteousness. The Holy Spirit our guide is the ever reliable, accurate, and consistent search engine that helps us determine our status per time—if we can be attentive and eager to make necessary adjustments.

> The Spirit Himself bears witness with our spirit that we are children of God, and if children, then heirs—heirs of God and joint heirs with Christ, if indeed we suffer with Him, that we may also be glorified together. (Romans 8:16–17 NKJV)

There is nothing that can be hidden from the Spirit of God, and there is no situation or information He does not have or He is not aware of. As stated in scripture,

> For the word of God is living and powerful, and sharper than any two-edged sword, piercing even to the division of soul and spirit, and of joints and marrow, and is a discerner of the thoughts and intents of the heart. And there is no creature hidden from His sight, but all things are naked and open to the eyes of Him to whom we must give account. (Hebrews 4:12–13 NKJV)

So we deceive ourselves when we think we can deceive God or that we can live a double life. He searches all things all the time and at all seasons. The book of Proverbs gives us an insight to the dynamics of this process:

> The spirit of a man is the lamp of the LORD, Searching all the inner depths of his heart. (Proverbs 20:27 NKJV)

In other words, God is for you; what remains is for you to show by your thoughts, words, and actions whether you are for Him. Jonah thought he could escape from the purpose and presence of God; well, you know the rest of the story. King David captures this appropriately in Psalm 139, where he says,

> Where can I go from Your Spirit? Or where can I flee from Your presence? If I ascend into heaven, You are there; If I make my bed in hell, behold, You are there. (Psalm 139:7–8 NKJV)

It's Not about Rowing Harder

In Jonah's case, we see that the seafarers initially tried to solve the problem by rowing harder to escape the adverse windy circumstance; they tried to no avail. Your solution does not necessarily lie in rowing harder or expending more physical energy but in doing proper analysis, asking relevant questions, and discerning your current situation.

The believer's battle is to continually check his motivation to determine whose interest and purpose is paramount; is it your personal interest or for the kingdom of God. Walking in line with your eternal purpose is the key to constant victory over life's adverse situations.

Jonah faced trouble as long as He was heading away from God; only the mercy of God saved Him from imminent destruction. The place of safety for the believer is the direction God directs. Having God on your side requires divine counsel, which the Spirit of God constantly provides to the believer. Our Lord Jesus, while addressing His disciples regarding the impending events and the ministry of the Holy Spirit, said,

> However, when He, the Spirit of truth, has come, He will guide you into all truth; for He will not speak on His own authority, but whatever He hears He will speak; and He will tell you things to come. (John 16:13 NKJV)

The first step to exiting a complex and adverse situation is to review where you are standing as well as the direction you are heading. There is no chaos or war that can stop the purpose of God. So the most valid question we must ask is 'Is God with me?'

He Desires to Enable Us to Fulfil His Purpose

God chose us before time, in our sinful state, but He desires to process us into what He has already appointed. God chose us; He had something in mind. The dynamics for each individual may be different, but the ultimate destination is bearing fruit that glorifies and exalts His name, fruit that will endure.

> You did not choose me but I chose you that you should bear fruit and that your fruit should remain. (John 15:16 NKJV)

He wants to be seen in us; we must be able to reflect His image and shine His light to a dying world. He chooses us, processes us, and equips us with the Holy Spirit to be His witnesses:

> But you shall receive power when the Holy Spirit has come upon you; and you shall be witnesses to Me in Jerusalem, and in all Judea and Samaria, and to the end of the earth. (Acts 1:8 NKJV)

What is God's will concerning my life? It is wisdom to trust and follow His lead at all times.

> Do not fear, little flock, for it is your Father's good pleasure to give you the kingdom. (Luke 12:32 NKJV)

We can be sure of one thing; God desires for us to succeed in what He commits into our hands. Our Lord gave us this assurance in the scripture referenced above. It is His good pleasure.

God is not your business partner; rather, He is your Master and Owner. He orchestrates our lives, and we owe Him obedience and service.

We must, therefore, understand that we belong to him.

When you come to the understanding that being a Christian is as a result of the manifold mercies of God, then you realize that it is an assured place where your past is unable to define the outcome of your future.

7

THE PROMISOR, THE PROMISE, AND THE CONDITIONS

> Whereby are given unto us exceeding great and precious promises: that by these ye might be partakers of the divine nature. (2 Peter 1:4 NKJV)

The Promisor, the Promise, and the Conditions are fused in one. The potency of the promisor guarantees the promise and enforces the attendant conditions. God is the Promisor and as the scripture above declares; His objective for laying out these promises is that we may become partakers of the divine nature.

Partaking in the divine nature means being restored to the original design intended from the beginning. He is our Father and like every good father; He would love for us to be like Him. So His expectation is that we should become gods as we respond and adjust to His Word and the leading of His Spirit.

In other words, the value of the promises become immeasurable when placed in their proper place; transforming mortal men to become like God.

I would like to add a caveat here: the promise of God is open to all but can only be appropriated by those who have committed to the journey with Him. This means that one who is living a life of sin should not be talking about the promises of God.

God encourages us to walk daily in these promises and to trust Him to do as He says. The primary condition is found in the book of Hebrews. He states as follows:

> But without faith it is impossible to please Him, for he who comes to God must believe that He is, and that He is a rewarder of those who diligently seek Him. (Hebrews 11:6 NKJV)

This scripture provides the foundation essential for any relationship or transaction with God. If you believe and expect God to fulfil His promises, you should also believe Him enough to live in obedience to His commandments.

> Therefore, leaving the discussion of the elementary principles of Christ, let us go on to perfection, not laying again the foundation of repentance from dead works and of faith toward God. (Hebrews 6:1 NKJV)

This makes it clear that repentance from dead works is completely foundational and should be firmly in place as one journeys deeper in God. It is faith in God that should propel repentance from dead works; there can be no valid faith in God while a person is comfortably living in sin.

> Little children, let no one deceive you. He who practices righteousness is righteous, just as He is righteous. He who sins is of the devil, for the devil has sinned from the beginning. For this purpose the Son of God was manifested, that He might destroy the works of the devil. (1 John 3:7–8 NKJV)

In the physical world, an inheritance is usually not validated until the one bestowing it dies. The reverse is the case with the promises of God; the beneficiary is required to die in order to inherit the promise.

The Word of God enjoins us to imitate those who have gone successfully before us and were able to inherit the promises through faith and patience. They all had to 'die' in a sense—not literally die but die to personal and selfish ambitions.

> But, beloved, we are confident of better things concerning you, yes, things that accompany salvation,

though we speak in this manner. For God is not unjust to forget your work and labor of love which you have shown toward His name, in that you have ministered to the saints, and do minister. And we desire that each one of you show the same diligence to the full assurance of hope until the end, that you do not become sluggish, but imitate those who through faith and patience inherit the promises. (Hebrews 6:9–12 NKJV)

Looking at the case of Abraham and the promise that God made to Him, the Bible states as follows:

Therefore from one man, and him as good as dead, were born as many as the stars of the sky in multitude— innumerable as the sand which is by the seashore. (Hebrews 11:12 NKJV)

Let us also review what our Lord Jesus Himself said regarding fruitfulness, which indeed applies to Him:

Most assuredly, I say to you, unless a grain of wheat falls into the ground and dies, it remains alone; but if it dies, it produces much grain. (John 12:24 NKJV)

Both portions of scripture apply to the realization of the promise of multiplication and increase. Please note that only healthy seed can be planted in expectation of fruit. The earth will swallow any unhealthy, infected, or diseased seed if it's planted. This makes the need for settling the matter of repentance from dead works before proceeding to the promises.

God has indeed given us great and precious promises which guarantee successful and fulfilled lives on earth. Realizing these promises is anchored on careful and diligent observance of embedded conditions. We see that being dead to self is a critical condition that must be fulfilled.

If Jesus did not die, God would not have exalted Him; Adam also had to be put to sleep before Eve could come. Most Christians are qualified for obtaining the promise, walking in obedience to God's will but they are still *too* alive for the essential work to be done in them.

Transformed by His Word

In the *Adventures of Tarzan* cartoon series, Tarzan grew up believing he was an ape because he was raised by apes and had adjusted himself to their lifestyle. He behaved in accordance with what he embraced and sought to be fully integrated in the society of apes.

We can only partake of the divine nature when we receive, embrace, and comply with the word of God, becoming pleasing to Him. When the word of God encounters one eager to adjust, it transforms him into the image of God, one step at a time.

God gave Abraham the promise but still took him through the process to test his trust and confidence in Him (Hebrews 6:12–18). Abraham passed the test because he was sold out totally. As a believer, I must hold unto God in every situation. We must count the word of God as superior to everything else.

> When Isaac asked his father for the lamb, Abraham answered his son: "My son, God will provide for Himself the lamb for a burnt offering." So the two of them went together. (Genesis 22:8 NKJV)

The way we live our lives reveal the extent to which we truly believe God. Be consistent in your boast concerning the good plans of God for your life and His ability to fulfil them. It doesn't matter if you are facing shame and reproach. As sure as morning follows night, the glory of God will be revealed. Remember that harvest comes after seed time.

Do not forget that the fulfilment of His promise is dependent on your determination to be true and unwavering to His requirements at all times.

> He sent His word and healed them, And delivered them from their destructions. (Psalm 107:20 NKJV)

You are delivered from every infirmity; the word of God is able to rescue us totally from every sin, debt, pressure, marital challenge, etc. We must keep our eyes on the Lord and not allow ourselves to be defined by the situations around us.

Stop Living for Yourself

If you are looking up to God to bless you on your own terms and by your timetable, you are living for yourself and are a hindrance to your progress. Believers must have God at the centre of their lives—determined to live for Him in love, truth, and obedience.

We must attain the point of total submission to God even to the point of death. Our motivation must be free of our personal opinion, preferences, and any other vested interests. As a principle, we must live our lives deliberately in line with God's will, becoming dead to ourselves.

Remember that the promise is sure and God desires that we become partakers of His divine nature; our response, therefore, must be in total surrender to God's will. Our hatred for every manner of sin indicates our readiness because only 'dead men' can inherit *his* promises.

8

CHOSEN FOR SUCCESS

It is futile and wasteful to profess Christianity, live out your years and never encounter the excellent and unimaginable power of God. Are you truly convinced that *He* is omnipotent, omniscient, and omnipresent? If the answer to that question is yes, it ought to be evidenced in your daily life and testimony.

By revelation the prophet Jeremiah cried thus:

> Ah, Lord GOD! Behold, You have made the heavens and the earth by Your great power and outstretched arm. There is nothing too hard for You. (Jeremiah 32:17 NKJV)

God is able and so powerful that accomplishing whatsoever He wills is nothing. In fact, He can make you into anything that He wants you to be; nothing can come close to stopping Him—except you. The reason for this is simple: He will not override your will.

The extent of His power is so immense and its scope so far removed from our comprehension that a mere peep into this vastness is only possible by His Spirit. When a man does what he says he will do, we say He has integrity. God is different; it is already done the moment He wills it, whether He speaks it or not. This is why the Bible tells us that it is impossible for God to lie.

> For men indeed swear by the greater, and an oath for confirmation is for them an end of all dispute. Thus God, determining to show more abundantly to the heirs

> of promise the immutability of His counsel, confirmed it by an oath, that by two immutable things, in which it is impossible for God to lie, we might have strong consolation, who have fled for refuge to lay hold of the hope set before us. (Hebrews 6: 16–18 NKJV)

In His dealing with Abraham, God truly wanted Abraham to become rested and have complete trust and confidence in Him. That Abraham may have strong consolation; to be assured that his hope in God is firmly and rightly placed. God swore by Himself since there is nothing greater, that the expectation of Abraham in Him would not fail.

Right from the beginning, God made man according to His image and likeness. Since He made us in His image, we should look and act like Him. Success, in our context, means accomplishing the reflection of God all around us, no matter the situation. Just as the fruit does not fall far from the tree, one who finds you should not be far from knowing God.

We learn from the scriptures that God is at liberty to use whatever pleases Him to bring about His plans and purposes. Instead of looking at celebrated and generally accepted people according to human and worldly standards, God prefers the base things that the world rejects. These base things are refined and processed into exactly what is required for His intended purpose.

Looking into the lives of some men and women, chosen by God to play roles in His unfolding eternal plan such as Abraham, Isaac, Jacob, Joseph, David and Gideon, we note that none of these men was well known or a celebrity when God chose him.

God chooses us irrespective of how rough or uncomely we are but does not leave us that way. The apostle Paul writing to the Corinthian Church said thus:

> For you see your calling, brethren, that not many wise according to the flesh, not many mighty, not many noble, are called. But God has chosen the foolish things of the world to put to shame the wise, and God has chosen the weak things of the world to put to shame the things which are mighty; and the base things of the world and the

things which are despised God has chosen, and the things which are not, to bring to nothing the things that are, that no flesh should glory in His presence. (1 Corinthians 1:26–29 NKJV)

That God chooses base things does not mean that God uses base things. He chooses us as we are, then begins the process of transformation from within us, which is essential for any role in His kingdom. He chooses what the world has rejected—because He is different from the world—but He never desires that whatever He chooses remain unchanged or unaffected.

Let us examine briefly some examples of men that God used at different times in pursuit of His purpose and plans, in order to see how He took them through the process.

Joseph

Sold into slavery as a teenager by his brothers because they were envious of their father's love and the dreams Joseph had and shared with them. He became a slave in the house of Potiphar. The Bible states as follows regarding Joseph's service in Potiphar's house:

> Now Joseph had been taken down to Egypt. And Potiphar, an officer of Pharaoh, captain of the guard, an Egyptian, bought him from the Ishmaelites who had taken him down there. The LORD was with Joseph, and he was a successful man; and he was in the house of his master the Egyptian. And his master saw that the LORD was with him and that the LORD made all he did to prosper in his hand. So Joseph found favor in his sight, and served him. Then he made him overseer of his house, and all that he had he put under his authority. (Genesis 39: 1–4 NKJV)

Joseph was well assured of his father's love and was not desirous of subsequent affirmation. His experience in His father's house had prepared him to trust God alone but to be also kind to other people. Joseph being conscious of the presence of God rejected the immoral overtures of Potiphar's wife and ended up in prison.

Not minding his own adversity and tribulations, he was extremely mindful of the countenance of others who were in a similar situation. His compassion for others is recorded as follows:

> Then the butler and the baker of the king of Egypt, who were confined in the prison, had a dream, both of them, each man's dream in one night and each man's dream with its own interpretation. And Joseph came in to them in the morning and looked at them, and saw that they were sad. So he asked Pharaoh's officers who were with him in the custody of his lord's house, saying, "Why do you look so sad today?" (Genesis 40: 5–7 NKJV)

Joseph's compassion for his fellow prisoners and his consciousness of the love and the presence of God prepared him for the office of Prime Minister of Egypt. A great part of this preparation, test, and confirmation took place while he was chief servant of Potiphar's household.

For truly, as our Lord Jesus said,

> He who is faithful in what is least is faithful also in much; and he who is unjust in what is least is unjust also in much. (Luke 16:10 NKJV)

Let me also remind you that Joseph was not sold into slavery for no reason; God had a plan to save the house of Jacob from an impending famine. He had also told Abraham that his descendants will be slaves in a foreign land and that He would deliver them with great substance after four hundred years:

> But God spoke in this way: that his descendants would dwell in a foreign land, and that they would bring them into bondage and oppress them four hundred years. (Acts 7:6 NKJV)

The dreams that Joseph had were truly aligned to the purpose of God. This purpose had to be established and all things visible and invisible were compelled to propel events in the direction of its actualization. The steps that Joseph's brothers took to ensure they didn't bow down to him, as he illustrated to them was to sell him into slavery. This act only helped the event come to pass. Such is the immeasurable and unsearchable wisdom and power of God.

Joseph was not oblivious of the purpose of God and the role determined for him in the scheme of things. This is evident in his conversation with his siblings after the death and burial of their father, Jacob.

> Then his brothers also went and fell down before his face, and they said, "Behold, we are your servants." Joseph said to them, "Do not be afraid, for am I in the place of God? But as for you, you meant evil against me; but God meant it for good, in order to bring it about as it is this day, to save many people alive. Now therefore, do not be afraid; I will provide for you and your little ones." And he comforted them and spoke kindly to them. (Genesis 50:18–21 NKJV)

Also, the Bible records that Joseph requested that his bones be exhumed when God takes them all back to the Promised Land. He knew there was more to his travails than the simple wickedness of envious siblings.

> And Joseph said to his brethren, "I am dying; but God will surely visit you, and bring you out of this land to the land of which He swore to Abraham, to Isaac, and to Jacob." Then Joseph took an oath from the children of Israel, saying, "God will surely visit you, and you shall carry up my bones from here." (Genesis 50:24–25 NKJV)

David

Jesse didn't reckon David as one of his promising sons. When Samuel came to his house as directed by the Spirit of God to anoint one of the sons of Jesse as king, in the stead of King Saul, David was not among the initial seven sons presented to the prophet.

> Thus Jesse made seven of his sons pass before Samuel. And Samuel said to Jesse, "The Lord has not chosen these." And Samuel said to Jesse, "Are all the young men here?" Then he said, "There remains yet the youngest, and there he is, keeping the sheep." (1 Samuel 16: 10–11 NKJV)

You know the rest of the story, how Samuel said he would not sit down until David arrived. On appearance, the Lord said to Samuel,

> And the Lord said, "Arise, anoint him; for this is the one!" (1 Samuel 16:12 NKJV)

Thus, when David had the opportunity to confront Goliath, he had this to say about the processing that had taken place in the wilderness:

> But David said to Saul, "Your servant used to keep his father's sheep, and when a lion or a bear came and took a lamb out of the flock, I went out after it and struck it, and delivered the lamb from its mouth; and when it arose against me, I caught it by its beard, and struck and killed it. Your servant has killed both lion and bear; and this uncircumcised Philistine will be like one of them, seeing he has defied the armies of the living God." Moreover David said, "The Lord, who delivered me from the paw of the lion and from the paw of the bear, He will deliver me from the hand of this Philistine." (1 Samuel 17: 34–37 NKJV)

David's case was so bad that Jesse his father did not consider inviting him for the anointing service. Today, David gives meaning to the name Jesse.

Gideon

At a time when the Jews were under severe and regular persecution and raids by the Midianites, the Israelites made for themselves dens, caves and strongholds. Gideon was threshing wheat in a cave when the angel of the Lord appeared to him:

> Now the Angel of the LORD came and sat under the terebinth tree which was in Ophrah, which belonged to Joash the Abiezrite, while his son Gideon threshed wheat in the winepress, in order to hide it from the Midianites. And the Angel of the LORD appeared to him, and said to him, "The Lord is with you, you mighty man of valor!" (Judges 6:11–12 NKJV)

The Lord went on to inform Gideon of His plan to use him to save Israel from the hand of Midian. Gideon was incredulous. He said to the Lord,

> So he said to Him, "O my LORD, how can I save Israel? Indeed my clan is the weakest in Manasseh, and I am the least in my father's house. (Judges 6:15 NKJV)

The Lord went on to assure him that the end is truly certain and the outcome determined.

> And the LORD said to him, "Surely I will be with you, and you shall defeat the Midianites as one man." (Judges 6:16 NKJV)

Gideon really felt inadequate and lacked confidence in himself. But no matter how inadequate and unqualified he felt, the call of God changed everything.

At the end of all this, the purpose determined by God was fulfilled through Gideon.

The Disciples of Jesus

Our Lord Jesus selected his disciples from different walks of life; most were fishermen and one a tax collector. They were not people who were reckoned with by the society of their time.

> And Jesus, walking by the Sea of Galilee, saw two brothers, Simon called Peter, and Andrew his brother, casting a net into the sea; for they were fishermen. Then He said to them, "Follow Me, and I will make you fishers of men." They immediately left their nets and followed Him. Going on from there, He saw two other brothers, James the son of Zebedee, and John his brother, in the boat with Zebedee their father, mending their nets. He called them, and immediately they left the boat and their father, and followed Him. (Matthew 4:18–22 NKJV)

These were regular folks going about their business before they met our Lord Jesus. Their proximity, daily interaction, and fellowship with Him transformed them so much that a few years later, the Bible records as follows:

> Now when they saw the boldness of Peter and John, and perceived that they were uneducated and untrained men, they marveled. And they realized that they had been with Jesus. (Acts 4:13 NKJV)

These were men who were ignorant, uneducated, and fearful but became transformed by the power of God. These men and others like them were instrumental to taking the gospel to the ends of the world at the risk of great personal peril.

God picks us as nobodies but transforms us into mighty tools and instruments in His hands. It is deception to accept mediocrity and excuse ourselves out of hard work, diligence and perseverance. You can be the best at what you do. No matter your state when He chose you, it is His plan to showcase you to the world.

You must be sure and bold, not shying away from the challenges consistent with being processed for His ultimate use. You can be holy, righteous, and prosperous. You can be in government, business, and every other legitimate sphere. As one chosen by the Lord, you should excel in any state or circumstance you find yourself.

God would choose you, no matter what state or condition you are in. Thereafter, with your cooperation, He transforms you into a vessel suited for His plans and purposes.

9

IN THE NAME OF JESUS

Most people use the name of Jesus for different purposes and objectives. It is used to start and end prayers, as exclamation as well as by comedians practising their art.

So, what does it mean to use the name of Jesus? The answer to this question is the subject of this chapter.

The name of Jesus is more powerful than you can imagine. It is more than an opening or closing statement used during prayers or a magic weapon chanted for petitioning heaven. It is also not the release of a sound, a test of pronunciation, a tool to reflect the degree of man's learning, or the last keyword in some magical process.

While speaking concerning Himself, our Lord Jesus said in answer to Thomas and the other disciples,

> Most assuredly, I say to you, he who believes in Me, the works that I do he will do also; and greater works than these he will do, because I go to My Father. And whatever you ask in My name, that I will do, that the Father may be glorified in the Son. If you ask] anything in My name, I will do it. (John 14:12–14 NKJV)

We can see clearly from this scripture that the Lord Jesus bestowed His name as an inheritance to a select group of people, those that believe in Him. In other words, only believers and followers of Jesus are licensed to use His name.

Every other use of His name is unlicensed, illegal and will not avail for such a person as desired. When His follower calls on His name or presents a petition to the Father in the name of Jesus; it is done.

He had told His disciples earlier on in the same chapter:

> I am the way, the truth, and the life. No one comes to the Father except through Me. (John 14:6 NKJV)

The potency and efficacy of the name comes from God's own authority as stated in Philippians 2:9 (NKJV):

> Let this mind be in you which was also in Christ Jesus, who, being in the form of God, did not consider it robbery to be equal with God, but made Himself of no reputation, taking the form of a bondservant, and coming in the likeness of men. And being found in appearance as a man, He humbled Himself and became obedient to the point of death, even the death of the cross. Therefore God also has highly exalted Him and given Him the name which is above every name, that at the name of Jesus every knee should bow, of those in heaven, and of those on earth, and of those under the earth, and that every tongue should confess that Jesus Christ is Lord, to the glory of God the Father.

The weight of authority in the Name of Jesus only responds to those who are licensed to exercise it. The 7 sons of Sceva in the Bible attempted to use the name of Jesus to cast out a demon, as they had seen the disciples do; the result was quite gory as,

> The man in whom the evil spirit was leaped on them, and overcame them, and prevailed against them, so that they fled out of that house naked and wounded. (Acts 19:14–16 NKJV)

For an individual to unlock the full potential and treasure resident in the name of Jesus, the following conditions have to be fulfilled:

Relationship

There must be a relationship between you and Jesus before you can use His name. Scripture states,

> As many as received him, He gave power to become the sons of God, even to them that believe on his name. (John 1:12 NKJV)

We receive Jesus by believing and accepting His Lordship over our lives and confessing with our mouths. We become His own not just because we say we are, but by being obedient to Him in all we do.

When you have a valid relationship with the Lord Jesus, everything created, visible and invisible understand and respond to this authority.

> Beware lest anyone cheat you through philosophy and empty deceit, according to the tradition of men, according to the basic principles of the world, and not according to Christ. For in Him dwells all the fullness of the Godhead bodily; and you are complete in Him, who is the head of all principality and power. (Colossians 2:8–9 NKJV)

Having a relationship with Jesus releases the power His name carries to change situations.

Revelation

When we have established our <u>relationship</u> with Christ, as we walk with Him, it is essential for us to have a <u>revelation</u> of Him. Understanding who He is in creation is essential to having the right perspective.

Speaking to the woman at the well of Samaria, our Lord Jesus said,

> If you knew the gift of God, and who it is who says to you, 'Give Me a drink,' you would have asked Him, and He would have given you living water. (John 4:10 NKJV)

So in addition to the relationship, we must have a revelation of Him. Our knowledge of Him through His Word enables commensurate authority and power when the name is used.

> That at the name of Jesus, every knee must bow of things in heaven of things in the earth. (Philippians 2:10 NKJV)

If Jesus lives in your heart, the spiritual beings understand and respect this by revelation.

The Purpose of the Name

In this world where sin and wickedness thrive, the name of Jesus is the viable and potent tool of enforcement that enables us to extinguish in totality the works of the devil,

> For this purpose the Son of God was manifested, that he might destroy the works of the devil. (1 John 3:8 NKJV)

The name of Jesus is infinitely effective and aligns everything to the very purpose of His manifestation.

The Duty of the Name

The name of Jesus has a divine mandate to perform and accomplish divine purpose in the life of a believer based on the relationship we have with Jesus,

> You did not choose Me, but I chose you and appointed you that you should go and bear fruit, and that your fruit should remain, that whatever you ask the Father in My name He may give you. (John 15:16 NKJV)

This shows us that Jesus takes responsibility for our lives because He chose us, and bestows us with his name for His glory. The name of Jesus is also tremendous equipment in the hands of the believer to perform wonderful acts.

The name of Jesus is a vital component of the corporation known as the kingdom of God. This Kingdom is poised and ready to reward faithfully in the life of anyone who works for the advancement of its purpose. Christians need to be ready to advance the kingdom of God; we need to start operating on that agenda. God is eager to lift you in the name of Jesus, not in your own name.

Every kingdom has its reward system; it should then not be surprising when the wicked seem to prosper in wickedness. What should concern the believer ought to be unlocking the immense treasures bestowed on him as an inheritance, which is largely un-utilized.

The scripture at the beginning of this chapter should spur us to very great heights. Our Lord Jesus said expressly that with the instrumentality of His name, those that believe Him would accomplish greater feats than He did. This is a muster call for every believer.

The name of Jesus is designed to answer at all times and to suffice for all situations.

10

THE TRUE DISCIPLE

How many people truly desire to be just like Jesus? The best and greatest height I can attain in the Kingdom is to be a true disciple; not a pastor, treasurer, evangelist or teacher.

Someone can be in any of these offices and not be a disciple; remember that Judas Iscariot was an apostle. The true test of the disciple is in how well he follows his master. Where you find the master you will also find his disciple.

The Church has many men and women who desire the offices but are indeed not disciples of Jesus. Most of these people have no appetite or true desire to be like Jesus in their daily pursuit; to be conformed to His image.

When God created man, He said, 'Let us make man in our image' (Genesis 1:26 NKJV). The world He made became broken at a point and His desired fellowship with man was disconnected, so He sent His Son Jesus to model the way for us to follow here on earth.

God is still in search of people He can transform into the image of His Son Jesus. God wants to have sons who reflect Him wherever they find themselves. The Lord said to Israel,

> For I am the LORD your God. You shall therefore consecrate yourselves, and you shall be holy; for I am holy.
> (Leviticus 11:44–45 NKJV)

He desires that His holy nature and revulsion for sin be seen in us as well.

Therefore, the summation of the work of the Holy Spirit in our lives is to make us look like Jesus.

> Therefore, if anyone is in Christ, he is a new creation; old things have passed away; behold, all things have become new. (2 Corinthians 5:17 NKJV)

The Spirit of Christ begins to work in us when we become born again. He works to enable us become dead to personal desires and ambitions. This begins the process of making us true and genuine disciples who take Jesus wherever we go. As stated earlier in this book, it is impossible to accomplish any of these without being dead to self, where God takes first place in our lives.

One of the easiest ways to confuse any set of people is to distort their goal or objective. Our goal as Christians should be to become like Jesus. Anything to the contrary is a major trap and a source of frustration. It is wise therefore to invest time in a diligent study of His life as recorded for us in scripture. He experienced total disregard and contempt from men many times in His sojourn on earth. However, this didn't bother Him at any point. He knew who He was and there was no need to seek any further validation. Many of us have committed ourselves to men. Our moods can be altered by what men do or fail to do.

So, in whatever situation you find yourself as you follow Jesus, it is wisdom to interpret the events with His own experiences as the background. Jesus fasted forty days and nights, and at the end was immediately tempted by the devil; afterwards, angels came and ministered unto Him (Matthew 4:11). This tells us to be resolute in exercising our faith, even when faced with adversity and tribulation; the Spirit of God is always waiting and ready to minister to us.

God Can Use You

The true disciple is the one that hears and dances to only heavenly drums. He has no hopes or expectations of special treatment and honour from men. Neither does he desire them nor does he take what men say to heart.

Ananias was introduced to us in the Bible simply as 'a certain disciple': 'Now there was a certain disciple at Damascus named Ananias; and to him the Lord said in a vision' (Acts 9:10 NKJV), meaning that God can use *anyone* ready (*not a particular person*) who is truly yielded to Him. You qualify to be used when you begin to fit the mould of men and women only motivated by the opinion of Heaven:

> For the eyes of the LORD run to and fro throughout the whole earth, to show himself strong in the behalf of [them] whose heart [is] perfect toward him. (2 Chronicles 16:9 NKJV)

God's eyes are not programmed to look in a particular place or direction. As we discussed earlier in chapter 7, as prophet Samuel arrived to anoint a King in Jesse's house as the Lord commanded, God's response to Eliab was

> Do not look at his appearance or at the height of his stature, because I have refused him. For the Lord does not see as man sees; for man looks at the outward appearance, but the LORD looks at the heart. (1 Samuel 16:7 NKJV)

'I have refused him' means that he was first considered but was eventually not chosen. My prayer is that you will be considered and chosen in the name of Jesus.

One of the strongholds of the enemy is *pre-disqualification*; where you encounter the promises of God in His word and immediately conclude that it cannot be you, believing that you are neither able nor deserving. Please know today that God can use you.

I am conscious and believe that my life and service is being recorded. So I am zealous to ensure that I write a good story by the choices I make daily. Could Ananias have known that we would be reading and learning from him today? We can live our lives rightly before God and be used in pursuance of divine plan and purpose.

Mary, the mother of Jesus, was chosen this way as well. There was nothing special about her; she was 'a certain virgin'. So have you disqualified yourself already? Change that mindset. God can use you too.

We must realize that God respects free will. Ananias could have refused God's request and 'another certain disciple' would have been used to restore Paul's eyes. God's promises must come to pass. All He is searching for is someone willing to align with Him. He keeps imploring us, giving us vital and cogent reasons why we ought to cooperate with Him.

During the famine, He sent prophet Elijah to be fed and sustained by a certain widow. The need of the prophet had to be met just as Paul's sight had to be restored. It is your choice to present yourself to Him to be used. God has made provisions for all men to be saved. Are you ready to be used in pursuit of that mandate? Do not disqualify yourself.

We can choose to become the game changers in our spheres of influence. Whatever the promise of God, we are qualified for it. These promises are not for theologians but for disciples, *the ones who discipline themselves continually* by following the Master, those who have overcome the pull of selfish ambitions and the thirst for personal glory.

Those certain, whom God saved, didn't do it for shame or mediocrity. God has chosen you so you can live a life of righteousness, holiness, integrity, and purpose, like Daniel, Mary, and Ananias. You can say to God, 'If you can use anything, use me,' and your request will surely be granted.

11

GENUINE WITNESSES

> And they went out and preached everywhere. (Mark 16:19–20 NKJV)

Have you ever narrated the resurrection story? Do the people around you understand what really happened at the cross? When an event takes place, the strength of that event is constrained or amplified by the actions of those who witnessed it and their testimony.

An event is only as significant as the witnesses' portrayal of it. An insignificant event can be made out as very significant by the witnesses because events on their own are primarily constrained by time and space.

The disciples were witnesses to the events of the cross and the ascension of Jesus Christ. They sought out opportunities and avenues to relate these experiences. Their collective effort is the singular reason we have the New Testament today.

To preach means to proclaim. It involves making bold declarations and spreading the good news of the gospel. The true definition of a witness is not just someone who sees an event but one who gives evidence or testifies to others. After all Christ has done, we cannot afford to keep quiet; we must publicize and give credence to these events and what they mean for us today.

Have you ever wondered that the gospel may be suffering for lack of credible witnesses? How can it be more interesting to expend our energy on things that have no eternal value—economy, politics, violence, longevity, sports, fashion trends, weight-loss programs, and the like—than on the good news of the cross? Why are we not broadcasting the availability of unlimited peace, joy, salvation, repentance, grace, and mercy?

We must become genuine witnesses of Christ by testifying of our faith to those we meet. These are some of the strategies to giving God first place in all that concern us. This includes making it our priority to implement what He desires to have implemented so that His will is done on earth as it is in heaven.

The great advantage of spreading the gospel is that the Lord will be with us, confirming His word with signs and wonders:

> And they went out and preached everywhere, the Lord working with them and confirming the word through the accompanying signs. Amen. (Mark 16:20 NKJV)

As children of God, we must learn how to boast in the Lord. According to the scriptures in Jeremiah,

> Then the Lord said to me, "You have seen well, for I am ready to perform My word. (Jeremiah 1:12 NKJV)

We have become too quiet about the gospel. We must begin to address situations around us and vehemently refuse anything that seeks to contradict the word of God. As our Lord Jesus commissioned His disciples and went out to proclaim the gospel, the Bible records that the following took place:

> So then, after the Lord had spoken to them, He was received up into heaven, and sat down at the right hand of God. And they went out and preached everywhere, the Lord working with them and confirming the word through the accompanying signs. Amen. (Mark 16:19–20 NKJV)

The Lord is eager to confirm His word in our lives, if we can declare with boldness all that Christ has done.

I have concluded that I will only say or repeat what God has said or what I understand to be His will. My advice to you today is this: *If God didn't say it, do not repeat it.* Have a personal policy to repeat only good news.

In the midst of the storm, when the disciples cried out in fear, Jesus rose up and rebuked the wind. He is always with His disciples. Do not fear!

When God finished all He did at creation, He took His rest and asked Adam to name the animals. He confirmed the names Adam gave the animals. There is a part for you in the divine plan of God, and He is eager to work with you to actualize it. He will never leave you to do it alone.

Genuine witnesses are not reticent; they are ready at all times to give first-hand information of an event. We must go from just observing the events of Christ's death to making the events reoccur in people's lives by telling them convincingly. The work of the Spirit is often discountenanced because believers are not quick and willing to testify. There is no Christian that would deny that Jesus died on the Cross. The problem lies in giving true evidence to this truth.

Jesus taught us a lesson when He proved that the power of God can deliver us from dead situations by raising Lazarus from the dead; we must trust God to keep us if we find ourselves in situations where we are unable to help ourselves. We must, therefore, endeavour not to limit ourselves to where our strength can take us, and we must believe God fully without natural or physical assurances.

In Acts 4:13 (KJV), the Bible states as follows:

> Now when they saw the boldness of Peter and John, and perceived that they were unlearned and ignorant men, they marvelled; and they took knowledge of them, that they had been with Jesus.

The critical factors expressed, therefore, are knowing Jesus and being with Jesus; apostle Paul puts it this way:

> That I may know Him and the power of His resurrection ... (Philippians 3:10 KJV)

> But if the Spirit of Him who raised Jesus from the dead dwells in you, He who raised Christ

from the dead will also give life to your mortal bodies through His Spirit who dwells in you (Romans 8:11 NKJV)

Paul and Peter had no natural basis for their output, yet people marvelled at them. They simply drew on the endowments of grace that God supplies. When we yield ourselves in total dependence to God, He knows how to work within us to achieve His purpose.

Part Three

Put Your Trust in God

12

DEPEND ON GOD

> Come to Me, all you who labor and are heavy laden, and I will give you rest. Take My yoke upon you and learn from Me, for I am gentle and lowly in heart, and you will find rest for your souls. For My yoke is easy and My burden is light. (Matthew 11:28–30 NKJV)

In our desire to place God first in everything and project an appropriate picture of Him as genuine witnesses, the enemy will surely try to discourage us.

Everyone places their trust and confidence in something or someone; so, who or what do you depend on? It is not for nothing that the Bible says,

> Some trust in chariots, and some in horses; But we will remember the name of the LORD our God. (Psalm 20:7 NKJV)

This tells us that people are prone to look for what to depend on, that a situation may arise that requires resources beyond what that individual or entity could provide.

Have you ever wondered why some problems are not solved? God has left nothing in the world without a provided solution; yet, not all problems are solved. This is an anomaly.

Part of the problem stems from the fact that problems are rarely paired with the appropriate and genuine solution. When you mismatch genuine need with a wrong solution, such as seeking to help yourself through the wrong channel, you commit sin. The fact that there is a genuine need or problem should lead us to find the genuine God-solution.

The devil continues to sell us the dummy that he loves us more than God, just as most teenagers prefer their peers' advice to that of their parents. It is only later in life, as they get older, that they become more appreciative of the love, instruction, and counsel of their parents. The same way, we should know better and should appreciate and depend on God's love in our lives.

God is good, loves His children and is eager to meet every genuine need. It behoves the believer to depend on God in every situation. Eve was deceived into believing that God was keeping the best from her; which is a lie still peddled by the adversary to date.

For everyone that is saved, God has invited each of us to a personal relationship with Him motivated by love. The reason Jesus says 'come to me' in our first scripture, is because He truly cares.

The power of God manifests when we match a genuine need with a correct expectation. So, rather than fret in the face of need or challenging situation, we should call unto God:

> Be anxious for nothing; but in everything by prayer and supplication with thanksgiving let your requests be made known unto God. (Philippians 4:6 NKJV)

Once we arrive at the conclusion that there is no other solution except in God, we are already on our way to overcoming the challenge.

Every satanic temptation is orchestrated to plant doubt and distract us from the Lord. The Word of God clearly outlines two evils commonly practised in the face of challenging circumstances:

> For my people have committed two evils; they have forsaken me the fountain of living waters, and hewed them out cisterns, broken cisterns, that can hold no water. (Jeremiah 2: 13 NKJV)

- *Forsaking the fountain of living waters.* The main strategy and objective of the devil is to divert and discourage us from fellowshipping with God. He knows he is powerless when the believer's trust is firmly anchored in God, so he works hard to distort things aiming to present God in a bad light. God will never disappoint those who put their trust in Him, as the Psalmist puts it:

> Those who trust in the LORD Are like Mount Zion, Which cannot be moved, but abides forever. As the mountains surround Jerusalem,
>
> So the LORD surrounds His people from this time forth and forever. (Psalm 125:1–2 NKJV)

Our God is a refuge from the storm and an ever-present help in time of need. The devil often succeeds in confusing people to seek solutions from the wrong places. He knows that for our God; it's all or nothing.

- *Digging out broken cisterns.* This can be likened to broken pots or sieves used in effort to fetch or store water, something they lack the capacity to do. A sieve is made with holes, while a broken pot has already been made ineffective for storing water. This entails abandoning the Lord for other options that are incapable of providing the assurances or performance desired.

  It can be self-comforting to be seen to be active, doing something about a situation in which you find yourself.

  Just bear in mind that no good thing can come from the devil; if it is not from the Lord, be sure it's from the devil. There are no middle grounds in spiritual matters.

God is jealous for us. He created us for His pleasure and expects to be our first and only dependable option when faced with difficulty. His jealousy creates a dependency on us to call upon Him through prayer, which ought to be our lifestyle.

We present to God every need both great and small for our sufficiency rests in Him. Therefore, difficulties should not threaten us; they are occasions for glory since the ends are certain.

Friends, God wants to gain glory through your challenge. Just hand it over to Him. There is nothing that excites a man like being confronted with a challenge he can handle. In the same way, when you have had the experience of overcoming every challenge that comes your way through your walk and interaction with God, you will not be afraid of trouble. God has called us to victory:

> For in all these things we are more than conquerors through him who loved us. (Romans 8:37 NIV)

Every person who is alive needs something to remain alive:

> And so it is written, the first man Adam became a living being; the last Adam became a life giving spirit. (1 Corinthians 15:45 NKJV)

Therefore, we can say a living being is a needing being and if we read this scripture in this light, it would read as follows: 'The first Adam was a needy being, while the last Adam became a need giving/supplying spirit.' As we know, it is more blessed to give than to receive.

Looking unto Jesus the author and finisher of our faith, to whom we are ambassadors, as the Bible says,

> As He is in this world so are we. (1 John 4:17 NKJV)

Jesus came to give us life from the life of God existing in Him and to destroy the work of darkness. Jesus did not live to consume but to give.

> Jesus came that we may have and enjoy life and have it in abundance to the full till it overflows (a rich and satisfying life). (John 10:10 AMP).

When we examine our lives, minimize our desires, and increase our giving, it becomes impossible for us to remain at the same level. We become powerful and godlike, operating above the things of the world.

The moment we come to the realization that our needs do not matter compared to what we can solve as life-giving spirits, we begin to enter an automatic alignment and become a channel that the Creator uses to meet the need of others.

Therefore, the secret to higher living is to stop focussing on our needs and connect with the source to discover a life that is satisfying and enriching.

Your heavenly Father is depending on you to encourage and lift someone out of his or her depression. As a life-giving spirit, you have been called to be a blessing, to raise those that have been bound by problems, to pray for the sick, to encourage, to give hope, and to dispense strength in righteousness.

God knows how to orchestrate events to favour you in ways you cannot imagine; many times, these packages come dressed as trouble or challenges.

13

Enjoy What You Have

> O LORD, You are the portion of my inheritance and my cup; You maintain my lot. The lines have fallen to me in pleasant places; Yes, I have a good inheritance. (Psalm 16:5–6 NKJV)

Are you embarrassed by what you consider to be a low and unfortunate state, with its attendant quality of life, in which you find yourself? Be careful lest your thoughts or actions portray you as one questioning his or her Creator's ability and intention.

Remember that some of the most affluent in the world today had humble beginnings or travelled through very challenging seasons. These were men and women who refused to allow their previous or current circumstances to determine their future.

In Genesis chapter 1, the earth that God created became void and formless, yet He proceeded to cause what He desired to come out of what had gone to ruins. This brought Him to verse 31, where He examined everything He had made and affirmed they were very good. So if we adopt this principle in our lives, we will be able to look back and appreciate how far we have come.

Our anchor scripture above tells us that it is God that maintains our lot, He is our portion. The circumstance that you find yourself is simply your allocation, which is not necessarily your destination. Rather, it is your starting point that will lead you to your end point. Faith does not deny where you are. Rather, it determines your current location and connects you to your desired location.

So we can say that God has not made a mistake concerning us since He knows our innermost desires. We need to understand that there is a process we must go through to get there. This is where it is important that we are convinced to trust in His goodness and accept the portion that has been allocated to us. This is the starting point. Wherever God has placed you currently is good; it is wisdom to enjoy it.

In the gospel according to John, our Lord Jesus, speaking concerning His imminent suffering and crucifixion, said,

> Shall I not drink the cup which my Father has given me. (John 18:11 NKJV)

We must be grateful for the 'cup', the portion He has allotted to each of us. One of the greatest deceptions the enemy uses is to make us focus on what we do not have, judging it to be better than what we currently have. Many of us have missed where God is taking us by not appreciating how far He has brought us.

The secret to Joseph's success was that even as a slave in Egypt, he enjoyed his work and made the most of what was committed into his hands. We see that he acted with dedication wherever he was placed, even in prison. He behaved as if he were already the prime minister before he got there. Potiphar's house was the dress rehearsal for the prime ministerial position of Egypt.

So, friends, take out time to enjoy where you are and what you have and appreciate the people around you. Spouses are the easiest to take for granted because of familiarity and proximity. They are often the first to be blamed when things go wrong as well as the last to receive credit when things go well.

The heart-breaking situation is when you see spouses comparing themselves to other couples, not appreciating each other. Constantly hounding each other and focusing on the other's shortcomings instead of their strengths. They fail to show kindness and assist the other in attaining desired adjustments where inherently necessary.

If only couples would commend each other deliberately and regularly—husbands loving wives while dwelling with them in wisdom and wives submitting to their own husbands in everything—then we would have more happy marriages.

We indict God when we judge what we have as not good enough. It can be easy to forget these essential lessons when the pressures of life build: before that happens, here are a few things to meditate on:

Be Content

The challenge of our lives is to be content with what we have at each stage of our lives.

> Godliness with contentment is great gain. (1 Timothy. 6:6 NKJV)

We must settle this in order to enter into the blessings reserved for us. You should not focus only on those things you do not have—expand your perspective.

Apostle Paul says, 'I have learnt in whatever state I am to be content with what I have' (Philippians 4:11 NKJV).

Accept Where God Has Placed You

Discontentment presents an inherent risk to what is yours; when you do not appreciate or value what you have, those who realize how valuable it is may take it from you.

At the garden of Eden, Eve was deceived by Satan to eat the forbidden fruit. He achieved this by painting an alluring picture of the possible outcome of eating the fruit. She failed to realize that God had already given her everything she thought would be provided by eating the forbidden fruit.

> Then the serpent said to the woman, "You will not surely die. For God knows that in the day you eat of it your eyes will be opened, and you will be like God, knowing good and evil. So when the woman saw that the

tree was good for food, that it was pleasant to the eyes, and a tree desirable to make one wise, she took of its fruit and ate. She also gave to her husband with her, and he ate." (Genesis 3:4–6 NKJV)

Recognize What You Have

When you recognize your portion, it helps you to enjoy it. Life does not require much to be enjoyed; it starts with deep appreciation of whatever you have in your current state and not despising the days of little beginnings.

It's important that you appreciate your spouse, children, colleagues, country, house, car, food, boss, and job. Enjoy everything God has given you and where he has placed you—these are the blessings of the Lord.

Be Thankful

Learn to say, 'Thank You, Lord' for your life every day. There is testimony in your current location. There is something to celebrate in it. Refuse to live in depression. The Psalmist said, 'Enter with the password: 'Thank you!' Make yourselves at home, talking praise. Thank him. Worship him' Psalm 100:4 (MSG).

That is the key to living life rightly, being appreciative of where the Lord has placed us, trusting in Him to take you to the destination He has purposed. Therefore, enjoy what you have and be content with where God has placed you while keeping an attitude of thanksgiving.

14

EMBRACE YOUR CALLING

Our society is shaped by people who have embraced, responded, and remained faithful to a calling—inventors, teachers, miners, pastors, missionaries, carpenters, engineers, doctors, researchers, scientists, and the like. These people have sacrificed their time, resources, and relationships to create discoveries and innovations to improve our societies. They are driven not by the pursuit of money or personal glory but by the need to better our societies.

Everyone on the surface of the earth was born with a specific purpose. At the time of Samson's birth, his father Manoah asked the angel,

> What is the child's purpose so that we can order him aright. (Judges 13:12)

True and lasting fulfilment comes with satisfying your divine purpose. Our most important quest must be to identify our purpose and fulfil it. Discerning your call is crucial for true satisfaction and fulfilment in life. Your call is that thing that gives you a sense of purpose, responsibility, or assignment. It must be clearly understood and beneficial to those around you.

> And we know that all things work together for good to them that love God, to them who are the called according to [His] purpose. (Romans 8:28 NKJV)

The true measure of success in the kingdom of God is comparing what

God intended for you with your accomplishments. It is not measuring your accomplishments against those of other people. Each person is designed to run a particular race and is equipped for their specific purpose. It is great folly to measure yourself by the standards of the world, particularly regarding worldly material acquisition.

The scripture above teaches that 'all things work together … to them who are the called according to [His] purpose'. This means that God makes all things work together for those who embrace their purpose.

Today, there is an overwhelming emphasis on the pursuit of personal ambitions and money. People are now being recognized and valued based on the volume of money they possess instead of what they contribute to society. This has become our pitfall, as societies are not advanced by the wealthy but by people who commit themselves to solving the problems that bedevil each generation of society.

Therefore, to identify our purpose and fulfil it, we must consider the following:

Be Born Again

Being born again is the starting point; salvation brings you to the defining moment on the journey towards the manifestation and the fulfilment of purpose. It gives direct access to the manufacturer, your Creator. Our Lord Jesus, speaking to Nicodemus, said as follows:

> Jesus answered, "Most assuredly, I say to you, unless one is born of water and the Spirit, he cannot enter the kingdom of God. That which is born of the flesh is flesh, and that which is born of the Spirit is spirit." (John 3:5 NKJV)

The Spirit holds the key to unlocking the purpose of every person born into the earth. You cannot attain your true purpose in God except He enables you to achieve it. The Spirit of God is the One at work in God's creation, fitting everything in its proper place.

No one else can give you clarity and understanding of your purpose in life and how to fulfil it except the Holy Spirit.

Discover Your Purpose

After the new birth, we must come to the realization that God has a plan for our lives. The new birth is not an end in itself. It is the beginning of an interesting and unending journey with God and in God.

Discern what God has raised you up to solve, and get on with it. What do you have a burden for? What do you see that you desire to change? That is a clear inkling to your calling, so work at it. Work is a blessing. There is dignity in labour.

Let us not buy into the frustration going on in the world today, where work has become spiteful and disgraceful. God says He will bless the works of our hands, so we must work.

When you realize your call, embrace it, whether it is profitable or not. Joseph is a classic example. While in Egypt, he served passionately wherever he was positioned, including the prison, Potiphar's house, and the king's palace. He was so effective at each stage of his call that the king had no choice than to place him in charge as prime minister. He was a problem solver; in today's parlance, he would be regarded as a consultant.

Understand Your Purpose

We must invest quality time to understand our calling if we intend to live purposeful lives. The priests asked John the Baptist, 'Who are you?'

> He answered, "I am the voice of one crying in the wilderness, make straight the way of the Lord." (John 1:23 NKJV)

John clearly understood his purpose; he knew that he was sent as the forerunner of Jesus, so he walked accordingly.

We are not called to the same thing, just as the mission and purpose of Jesus was different from that of John the Baptist. When you understand your call, it takes a superior position over whatever discomforts you encounter on the way.

Embrace Your Purpose

You can only fulfil your purpose and calling in life after you discover, understand, and work at it.

> Let each one remain in the same calling in which he was called. (1 Corinthians 7:20 NKJV)

We must realize that people rarely make money by setting out to make money. Money rightfully answers to the fulfilment of purpose and solution to people's problems.

Immense wealth and prosperity can only be acquired by people who do not set the acquisition of wealth as their initial target but are motivated by a desire to embrace their purpose. As long as you are in your place of assignment, doing what you should do to be a blessing to others, keep at it, because wealth and fulfilment is certain.

Life is much more than the things you are pursuing, true prosperity and fulfilment comes from fulfilling purpose. If everyone fulfilled their purpose, many of the problems bedeviling mankind would be solved.

Everyone must, therefore, embrace their purpose; by first being born again, discerning their purpose, and taking out time to understand, embrace, and run with it.

Remember that *all things work together for good to them that embrace their purpose.*

15

THE PRINCIPLE OF MERCY PROBLEMS

In 2 Kings 3:4, we see the beginning of a very dramatic sequence of events, akin to the stuff of blockbuster movies. A rebellion by a king who had hitherto paid tributes to the king of Israel led to a mustering of troops and activation of military alliances to an expected epic battle.

> Now Mesha king of Moab was a sheepbreeder, and he regularly paid the king of Israel one hundred thousand lambs and the wool of one hundred thousand rams. But it happened, when Ahab died, that the king of Moab rebelled against the king of Israel. (2 Kings 3:4–5 NKJV)

In the midst of delay and being lost in the wilderness for seven days; it came to clear realization that they had no water for troops, animals, or anyone else.

> So the king of Israel went with the king of Judah and the king of Edom, and they marched on that roundabout route seven days; and there was no water for the army, nor for the animals that followed them. (2 Kings 3:9 NKJV)

This caused Jehoshaphat to ask for the intervention of God through the prophet. The reassuring Word of God came through the prophet Elisha from verse 16, bringing a solution to their problem.

> And he said, "Thus says the LORD: 'Make this valley full of ditches.' For thus says the Lord: 'You shall not see wind, nor shall you see rain; yet that valley shall be filled with water, so that you, your cattle, and your animals may drink.' And this is a simple matter in the sight of the LORD; He will also deliver the Moabites into your hand. Also you shall attack every fortified city and every choice city, and shall cut down every good tree, and stop up every spring of water, and ruin every good piece of land with stones." (2 Kings 3:16–19 NKJV)

The human body is designed with lots of defence mechanisms, and certain symptoms are meant to indicate more serious underlying conditions. Fevers, colds, and catarrh fall within this category for most individuals and usually indicate that the individual should take time out to rest. Mercy problems are like those mild indicators prodding us to the realization that all is not well.

In the developing plot, the same conditions and circumstances caused King Jehoram and King Jehoshaphat to arrive at different interpretations and conclusions based on the meditations of their hearts. King Jehoram felt that God was out to destroy him and others, while King Jehoshaphat knew that the only way out was in God.

> And the king of Israel said, "Alas! For the LORD has called these three kings together to deliver them into the hand of Moab." But Jehoshaphat said, "Is there no prophet of the LORD here, that we may inquire of the LORD by him?" So one of the servants of the king of Israel answered and said, "Elisha the son of Shaphat is here, who poured water on the hands of Elijah." And Jehoshaphat said, "The word of the LORD is with him." So the king of Israel and Jehoshaphat and the king of Edom went down to him." (2 Kings 3:10–12 NKJV)

Our judgment of God will always express itself in our thoughts, words, and actions. The prophet intervened out of respect for the person of Jehoshaphat and prophesied as recorded in scripture:

> And he said, "Thus says the LORD: 'Make this valley full of ditches.' For thus says the LORD: 'You shall not see wind, nor shall you see rain; yet that valley shall be filled with water, so that you, your cattle, and your animals may drink.' And this is a simple matter in the sight of the LORD; He will also deliver the Moabites into your hand." (2 Kings 3:16–18 NKJV)

The Lord promised to send a miraculous flow of water in a way that had never been known, seen, or heard before then. If that were the only thing that their visit to the prophet accomplished, it would have been enough.

When we recall that the dearth of water for men on a military campaign is actually a death sentence, the importance of thanksgiving at the miraculous replenishment of water would be clear to everyone in Israel.

However, the last verse of the scripture referenced above introduces an extension or twist to the miracle, which was outside the scope of their current problems. It says,

> And this is a simple matter in the sight of the LORD;
> He will also deliver the Moabites into your hand. (2 Kings 3:18 NKJV)

Some of the challenges we come across in life are actually designed to bring us out of potentially more destructive future situations. The major issue that propelled these three kings was to battle the people of Moab into submission and compel them back into subjugation to Israel. But the immediate challenge that caused them to seek God was to get a solution to the near-fatal scarcity of water.

It follows that it would have been devastating if the scarcity of water hit them in the midst of battle; so this indicates that the seven-day delay was helpful to them. They would have been faint and surely lost the battle if the scarcity hit in the midst of fighting.

It is also possible that their victory in that battle was orchestrated by coming to God through the prophet Elisha, which would not have happened if there had been no scarcity of water. Many of the challenges we come across in life are actually designed to save us from imminent calamity.

So mercy problems are those challenges that come our way, mostly orchestrated by God to save us from future calamity. Understanding this principle is essential for us to be able to 'rejoice always, pray without ceasing, in everything give thanks; for this is the will of God in Christ Jesus for you' (1 Thessalonians 5:16–18 NKJV).

When a believer is firm and honest in his convictions, the presence of trouble in his life is usually to save him from bigger and more destructive trouble ahead. This is why we must not mourn, think, or confess like the world. Our case is different.

16

CAMOUFLAGE OF BLESSING

I know you must have encountered challenging situations that seem to get more difficult as you pray? In some cases, the more you tried to unravel the complexity of the problem, the more it acquired additional complexity and energy. Confronted with this sort of scenario, many believers have quietly wondered, *but how can I be going through this when God is all-powerful?*

It is rare for you to find the blessings of God simply presented as blessings. If the five thousand people that Jesus fed all came with their lunch for the meeting, would they have had any leftover after feeding? The scarcity of food and only five loaves of bread and two fish left twelve baskets of food. So in the way and manner God works, most times blessings come our way camouflaged as problems. It is not for nothing that scripture asserts that, 'the just shall live by faith' (Hebrews 10:38).

Most of those that God used mightily were children whose births were preceded by pain, frustrations, fears, and thoughts of disappointment. Samuel the prophet is case in point; his mother was called barren and had wept for years before he was conceived.

Isaac was conceived a whole twenty-five years after God promised Abraham that he would have a son born to him. But whenever their stories are recounted today, there is great rejoicing for their beginning. Truly, as the Bible declares, 'better is the end of a thing than the beginning thereof' (Ecclesiastes 7:8 KJV).

Knowing the intent and purpose of God concerning you should strengthen you in the face of trouble.

God states this in His Word:

> For I know the thoughts that I think toward you, saith the LORD, thoughts of peace, and not of evil, to give you an expected end. (Jeremiah 29:11 KJV)

In a different but similar verse, He states as follows:

> For my thoughts are not your thoughts, neither are your ways my ways, saith the LORD. For as the heavens are higher than the earth, so are my ways higher than your ways, and my thoughts than your thoughts. (Isaiah 55:8–9 KJV)

Now the word of God clearly describes the sovereignty of God and the greatness of His power as God—omnipotent (He can do all things), omniscient (He knows all things), omnipresent (always present); but He beclouds information concerning His ways:

> He made known his ways unto Moses, his acts unto the children of Israel. (Psalm 103:7 KJV)

It is wisdom for us then to discover and learn the ways of God in order to appreciate His power. God is taking us on a journey and knows the best route to take. Quite often, when we expect Him to take the highway, He changes the course in our best interest; it may explain neither the route nor the reason for the change. Let us liken it to expecting a pilot to describe the flight route to you as a passenger on his aircraft. His explanation may really offer you no help, assuming he does at all, so all we need to do is to trust that he knows the way through the skies.

In the same way we must come to the realization that God can do all things and He must be trusted to work it out His own way. This is essential for our faith, as Hebrews 11.6 states,

> But without faith it is impossible to please Him, for he who comes to God must believe that He is, and that He

is a rewarder of those who diligently seek Him. (Hebrews 11:6 NKJV)

So essentially, our Faith states that we have no confidence in things as they appear. This means that whatever we see is *suspect* and that only the Word of God is the *anchor* to hold, no matter the situation, whether good or bad.

Second Chronicles 20:1–21 opens with an interesting story. We see Jehoshaphat faced with war from three different nations at the same time. He took out time to seek the Lord; the Spirit of God assured him through Jahaziel that the battle belonged to God, that there was no need for Jehoshaphat to fight in the battle. The Lord encouraged him to position himself, stand firm, and see the salvation of the Lord.

> Then the Spirit of the LORD came upon Jahaziel the son of Zechariah, the son of Benaiah, the son of Jeiel, the son of Mattaniah, a Levite of the sons of Asaph, in the midst of the assembly. And he said, "Listen, all you of Judah and you inhabitants of Jerusalem, and you, King Jehoshaphat! Thus says the Lord to you: 'Do not be afraid nor dismayed because of this great multitude, for the battle is not yours, but God's. Tomorrow go down against them. They will surely come up by the Ascent of Ziz, and you will find them at the end of the brook before the Wilderness of Jeruel. You will not need to fight in this battle. Position yourselves, stand still and see the salvation of the Lord, who is with you, O Judah and Jerusalem!' Do not fear or be dismayed; tomorrow go out against them, for the Lord is with you. (2 Chronicles 20:14–17 NKJV)

In other words, God was saying, 'You will not need to fight but neither will you draw back nor be afraid of them.' The Lord said, 'Tomorrow go out against them' because the Spirit that we have is the Spirit of Sonship and boldness (we are not cowards). We step out in obedience, whether we know what to do or not, for we are well assured that the Commander-in-Chief knows what to do.

As they stepped out in the morning in the face of war, we also see Jehoshaphat's attitude; he appointed singers who should praise the beauty of God's holiness, singing, 'Praise the Lord, for His mercy endures forever!' They chose to sing praise songs as their war song in the face of serious trouble.

This should teach us something about our confession. Often times we praise God because of our experience, which is a level of praise. But when we praise God based on our revelation of His person, that is a higher level that is superior to any experience.

Many of us profess to believe in God, but our speech betrays us. As believers, we should be careful how we comment in the face of trouble. We are not commentators; rather, we are priests who declare the counsel of the Lord at all times. The Bible states thus in Isaiah 54:17,

> "No weapon formed against you shall prosper, And every tongue which rises against you in judgment You shall condemn. This is the heritage of the servants of the LORD, And their righteousness is from Me," Says the LORD. (Isaiah 54:17 NKJV)

We should stand to bring God's purpose and Kingdom down and shift things into their proper positions. Our greatest weapon of battle is our own obedience to God. When we are fully submitted, it becomes a walkover to compel circumstances in disarray to come into alignment. The Bible says in the book of James,

> Submit yourselves therefore to God. Resist the devil, and he will flee from you. (James 4:7 NKJV)

We are the priests connecting divinity to humanity; we must be conscious of our role. Do not be a commentator; rather, be a priest.

> So when men are cast down, then thou shalt say, there is lifting up. (Job 22:29 KJV)

The Bible also records that as Jehoshaphat and his people began to sing and to praise, the Lord set an ambush against the armies that came out against him and defeated them all completely. When the people of God came to take away the spoil, they found an abundance of riches and precious jewels.

So, we see that the 'great army' coming against Jehoshaphat earlier in the scripture was armed with valuables and treasures for Jehoshaphat's blessing and their weapons of war were of no consequence.

As a child of God, once you are sure that you are in obedience to God, doing all He has commanded of you and trouble comes, be assured that the trouble is a blessing dressed in camouflage.

For example, someone may be working in an organization and, by reason of righteousness, lose the job. This may become the doorway to becoming an entrepreneur. Or a married couple faithfully doing God's will may experience a delay in childbirth. Hold on. Your blessing is right at the corner, dressed as a problem.

Do not give undue credit to the devil. When he needed to afflict Job, he had to ask God for permission. This tells us that there is a leash on him and that how far he can go is already determined.

Joseph said to his brothers,

> But as for you, you meant evil against me; but God meant it for good, in order to bring it about as it is this day, to save many people alive. (Genesis 50:20 KJV)

God is orchestrating that problem for a blessing; your informed praise of God unveils and unwraps the gift hidden in the problem. Thanksgiving is what unbuttons the camouflage so you can see the blessing in it.

> Be anxious for nothing; but in everything by prayer and supplication with thanksgiving let your requests be made known unto God. (Philippians. 4:6 NKJV)

If you knew what God had for you in that situation, you will repeat the song of Jehoshaphat: *Praise the Lord for His mercy endures forever.*

We understood and came to a conclusion in the course of our Church auditorium building project that *every problem has a solution*. It is futile for us to hope that problems and challenges will not arise, the only way out is to ask God for the solution.

In fact, some problems or challenges you currently face are divinely initiated so that the Glory of God may be made manifest. Are you ready to ignite an ambush against everything negative in your life? Just as Jehoshaphat received the news of the armies coming against him, you can change the outcome by agreeing with God, to see an unveiling of that camouflage as a true blessing orchestrated by God.

17

WHERE HAVE YOU LAID HIM?

The story of Lazarus is one that most of us are very familiar with in the New Testament. It's an account of a very popular family, which opened with a sick Lazarus. His sickness was so severe that word was sent to Jesus that He was indeed very sick.

> Now a certain man was sick, Lazarus of Bethany, the town of Mary and her sister Martha. It was that Mary who anointed the Lord with fragrant oil and wiped His feet with her hair, whose brother Lazarus was sick. Therefore the sisters sent to Him, saying, "Lord, behold, he whom You love is sick." When Jesus heard that, He said, "This sickness is not unto death, but for the glory of God, that the Son of God may be glorified through it." (John 11:1–4 NKJV)

Our Lord Jesus had a very cordial relationship with this family and often would visit and fellowship with them. So the message, which was sent to Jesus, had to inform Him that it was the one whom He loved that was ill.

In the natural order, it would have been inconceivable that Jesus, who had healed all and sundry, would tarry for this long after hearing that one so dear to Him was ill. But He made a profound statement to His disciples. He said, 'This sickness is not unto death.'

The Lord always knows what to do and when to do it. We must never forget this truth. We understand that where Jesus was at the time required a full day's journey from Bethany. This meant that the emissary took two days to get to Jesus and return to Bethany.

When Jesus arrived after two extra days, He found that Lazarus was already dead and buried for four days. It is unclear if and how long they waited for our Lord Jesus before deciding to bury Lazarus.

Martha said, 'If you had been here he would not have died.' That sounded as if she was accusing Jesus instead of looking up to Him; judging Him for not leaving whatever else needed to be attended to in order to make it in time to forestall the death of Lazarus.

Like most of us, she forgot that whenever God shows His hand in any situation is the best possible time.

There are many lessons to learn from this account. A critical lesson is the importance of not burying your dreams and aspirations, especially those things you committed to God or received from Him, without giving Him the final say.

There are many kinds of graves where dreams are laid, but no matter their kind or description, they serve a common purpose of bringing something to finality before the desired objective has been achieved.

It may be helpful for you to review those dreams and visions that the Lord planted in your heart at the beginning of your walk with Him—specific callings dear to His heart, such as using your gifting to spread the gospel of Jesus and win souls into His kingdom.

Find where you laid your dreams—and bring them back to life.

18

ACCURATELY WAITING ON GOD

When you read the Bible, some statements are categorical, statements that are absolute and provide no room for dialogue. These statements are intended to serve as anchors, beacons, or compasses, pointing out the right direction for us to follow.

> Since the beginning of the world men have not heard nor perceived by the ear nor has the eye seen any God besides you our God who acts for the one who waits for Him. (Isaiah 64:4 NKJV)

Verse 5 goes further to say, 'You meet him who rejoices and does righteousness. Who remembers you in your ways.'

The Bible is stating that our God has a *reputation*.

Isaiah 49:23–25 NKJV says, 'They shall not be ashamed who wait for me.'

When you wait on the Lord, it is impossible for you to be ashamed at the end of the day. God is omnipotent, omniscient, and omnipresent; there is nothing our God cannot do.

Praise addresses the situations in our lives by helping us get the right perspective of God and properly align with Him. It helps us see a better picture of the Most High; He is the God with whom there is no variableness, no shadow of turning, no darkness, no mistake with Him—what He is He is.

We all need an active and secure connection with God, which goes beyond Church attendance. Looking at the scriptures, we find a connecting point between God and His people. That point is enclosed in the word 'waiting'.

Philippians 4:6 admonishes us to 'be anxious for nothing'. Waiting can be seen as not being anxious; waiting means trusting, and you can submit only when you trust.

When you are at peace with where you are and the circumstances that surround you, your performance will be greatly enhanced. So we all have to work to attain genuine peace.

> Blessed is the man who trusts in the Lord ... For you shall be like tree planted by the rivers of waters.' (Jeremiah 17:7–9 NKJV)

Every imagery God uses is for a purpose. Just as the tree that is planted cannot change position; a man planted is settled even when he is facing adverse situations.

The problem we have is that while we are waiting on God, we allow ourselves to be drawn in different directions and attracted by different alternatives thereby missing our hour of visitation. To be like a tree planted is to be open and ready for heat coming from above and water coming from beneath.

There is no reason to fear because, like the tree, the man is connected to the water and minerals and open to sunlight. Our goal is to be men and women whose trusts are in the Lord, not being anxious or apprehensive. This makes it possible for us to yield fruit all year round.

Using the illustration of the feeding of five thousand men with five loaves and two fish, God gave us an insight.

Our Lord Jesus said to the disciples to *make* the people sit down; that is, to compel them to sit down before they were miraculously fed. This indicates to us that not much would have been achieved in a state of anxiety and disorder.

If you are truly a child of God, He knows your location and will send your miracle your way. There is no need for you to run from pillar to post.

On the other hand, some people use waiting on God as an excuse for laziness and slothfulness, making the name of God appear ineffective.

People who understand that waiting on God requires attentiveness can control their thoughts, speech, and actions. God is faithful, and we should maintain our focus on Him and avoid every form of distraction.

19

GOD WILL NOT FORGET

Why do people do the things they do? Why do people commit immoral acts, armed robbery, kidnappings, fraud, murder, etc.? Why are they so conveniently and easily lured into disobedience? Why are people quick to yield to temptation and even scorn those determined to obey God?

Since heaven is neither for the rich nor poor but for the righteous, why do people do the ungodly things they do?

They do these things because they have been deceived into believing that they can escape the consequences of their actions.

James 4:7 (NKJV) admonishes as follows: 'Therefore submit to God. Resist the devil and he will flee from you.'

The passage of scripture from Esther 2:21 into 3:1 follows a background of King Xerxes and Queen Vashti. This queen refused the king's summons! Imagine that!

Did she perhaps forget her duties as a queen? Her responsibilities? Queen Vashti failed to understand that life is warfare. She was slack in her obligations, forgetting how powerful her King was. If she had known …

The fact that one gets away with something one day is no guarantee of the continuity of this state of affairs. God is slow to anger but abounding in mercy. We need to remember there is a war going on. It takes wisdom and faithfulness to prosecute and be active in a state of warfare.

This story in the book of Esther introduces Mordecai—an advantageously placed scribe and an official in King Xerxes's court. He was loyal to God. He was privileged to hear a plot by two soldiers against the king's life. This was made known to the king in Mordecai's name through his cousin Esther, who was now Queen. The punishment was meted out to the plotters immediately. The reward for revealing the coup was a recording in the annals of the King; nothing seemingly tangible was done for Modecai.

Ecclesiastes 8:11 (KJV) states as follows:

> Because the sentences for evil work is not executed speedily therefore the heart of the sons of men is fully set in them to do evil.

Perhaps our world could have been a better place if there was rapid response for evil—an immediate reckoning. Because humans are creatures of time, the lack of immediate punishment causes insensitivity to the wages of sin.

> With the merciful You will show Yourself merciful; With a blameless man You will show Yourself blameless, With the pure You will show Yourself pure; And with the devious You will show Yourself shrewd. (Psalm 18:25–26 NKJV)

This scripture above reminds us that God will be merciful with the merciful, with the upright He will be upright, with the pure He will be pure, with the devious He will show Himself shrewd.

> For God is not unjust to forget your work and labor of love which you have shown toward His name, in that you have ministered to the saints, and do minister. (Hebrews 6:10 NKJV)

God will definitely reward even if circumstances and events make it seem like he has forgotten. Note that it seemed God had forgotten in the case of Mordecai.

After this, the next line points to the appointment of Haman the Agagite, and Mordecai is 'forgotten'. Esther 3:2 even continues that some uncommon honour came along with this promotion; everyone was compelled to bow before Haman by decree of the king; Mordecai would have none of it.

Who knows? Perhaps Haman even needed the backing of the king to receive any respect as a result of personal despicable character traits. What was Mordecai's reason? The Bible is silent on this, but did Mordecai perhaps discern something unholy, corrupt, or undeserving of such respect? Or for the simple reason of the first commandment, being separated as a Jew. Esther 3:6 states that Haman was so furious he determined not to punish Mordecai only but to eliminate all Jews.

In verse 7, Haman and his cohorts chose a date after casting lots (divination). However, they were ignorant of the fact that Proverbs 16:33 (NKJV) states:

> The lot is cast into the lap, but it's every decision is from the LORD.

He was also unaware that, "there are many plans in a man's heart/ Nevertheless the LORD'S counsel—that will stand" (Proverbs 19:21 NKJV).

Mordecai was not privy to all the conniving and plotting until a decree went out with the King's seal approving the total annihilation of all Jews. Esther 3:15 tells us that the king and Haman then went to drink "… while the whole of Shushan (where the Jews reside) was perplexed" (Esther 3:15 NKJV).

Mordecai refused the covering that Esther sent him, choosing to stand with the Jews. He warned Esther not to be deceived into thinking she might escape. Mordecai perceived more than the present—how far-reaching the consequences of such a decree could be.

Alas! God overthrew the wicked plans of Haman against the Jews, by causing the king to lose sleep and call for the records. He remembered that nothing had been done for Modecai as compensation for saving the king's life. The dynamics of events became altered in favour of Modecai and the Jews.

God is faithful! He alone knows when He will reward you. Is the enemy telling you the contrary? That God has forgotten your labour of love? God cannot forget.

Hezekiah prayed and received healing according to his desires, but my prayer is for God to answer me according to His riches in glory, not because of my desires but because of his desires for me.

Remember in Joseph's life, in Genesis 40:23: for two years, that butler forgot, but God caused him to remember at the right time. God's due season will surely come. Do not even be deceived by others with sudden or spectacular breakthroughs.

There is still a reward for good, for righteousness and waiting on the Lord. There is recompense for evil too.

> See, I have inscribed you on the palms of My hands;
> Your walls are continually before Me. (Isaiah 49:16 NKJV)

The word of God makes it clear that God has carved us in the palm of His hand and can *never* forget. Keep doing good! Keep living in righteousness and sowing good seeds. God never forgets!

Part Four

Put Your Faith to Work

20

INCREASING FAITH—BY REASON OF USE

Faith increases with the way we respond to challenging opportunities that present themselves before us. Every situation we face is an opportunity to live by faith or to compromise.

> Now the just shall live by faith: but if any man draws back, my soul shall have no pleasure in him. (Hebrews 10:38 NKJV)

The level of your faith today is a measure of how you exploited the opportunities that were presented to you. The challenges we face daily are actually opportunities to trust God or to call Him untrue. When you become consistent in overcoming these challenges; your faith in God is built up and very strengthened. A classic example is believers who become used to tithing. They know by experience that things are easier when they return their tithe out of reverence to God and not out of coercion or fear. Scripture states,

> Bring all the tithes into the storehouse, That there may be food in My house, And try Me now in this," Says the LORD of hosts, "If I will not open for you the windows of heaven And pour out for you such blessing That there will not be room enough to receive it." (Malachi 3:10 NKJV)

There are so many areas in our lives where increased faith is essential, such as our health and wellbeing, business, giving, living, etc. Those who prove God, who respond in faith, know that He always comes through faithfully. No man has ever stepped out on a limb for God and experienced failure.

However, if you never step out, you cannot experience His miraculous works. The tendency will be for you to be tempted to believe that God will fail you. The only way to overcome this is to step out.

The devil is so cunning; he knows how to give you reasons to draw back, telling you all the potential problems that can arise. However, the only way to grow in faith is to seize situational opportunities that present themselves.

> Those who by reason of use have their senses exercised to discern both good and evil. (Hebrews 5:14 NKJV)

Ownership does not correspond to usage, and benefit is not necessarily derived from ownership. The fact that you own something does not mean it benefits you. Many of us have things we own but do not use. To use simply means to *employ something for purpose*. Whatever you do not use or exercise is unlikely to grow. Use means to do something habitually. The Christian is a practiser. Christianity grows and strengthens through practice.

It is amazing how a wrecked person, after accepting Christ, becomes changed radically by consistently attending a Bible class or discipleship meeting, where he is constantly engaged in the word of God. After a while, those hours invested in habitually re-ordering his mind will produce an enormous change, making him mighty in God's hand. Some of us have made habits of things that cannot help us; yet we are waiting for God to move in our situation.

To derive reasonable benefit from any skill, time and diligence are essential. You can dedicate time to study God's word habitually, excitedly waiting for Him to speak to you through His Word.

> Day unto day utters speech, And night unto night reveals knowledge. (Psalm 19:2 NKJV)

Jesus described this scenario in the parable of the sower when He stated as follows:

> And these are they likewise which are sown on stony ground; who, when they have heard the word, immediately receive it with gladness; And have no root in themselves, and so endure but for a time: afterward, when affliction or persecution arises for the word's sake, immediately they are offended. (Mark 4:16–17 KJV)

A plant can be standing, but if it is not deep-rooted, it will exist only for a short while. Deep roots ensure longevity. Same way, when you hear a message on prudence, giving, marriage, or habit, if you do not determine immediately to begin to practise and prove it, what you heard will bring you no benefit; it will be stolen from your heart.

Another parable that illustrates this is the parable of the talents, in Matthew 25:15–30 (NKJV):

> For the kingdom of heaven is like a man traveling to a far country, who called his own servants and delivered his goods to them. And to one he gave five talents, to another two, and to another one, to each according to his own ability; and immediately he went on a journey.

You may have just one talent today, but putting that talent to judicious use will cause more talents to be added. But if you choose to neglect or bury it; be sure it will be given to the man with more talents who knows how to utilize. Faith is accepting what is available and putting it to faithful use. The faithfulness of God will see your obedience and will bless that talent and cause it to multiply in your hands.

To obey God is a risk we must be able to take knowing that God is looking to increase the capacity of those who risk the most in His name.

In the parable of the talents, we get an opportunity to see this principle in action. The master commanded as follows:

> 'Take the thousand and give it to the one who risked the most. And get rid of this "play-it-safe" who won't go out on a limb. Throw him out into utter darkness. (Matthew 25:28 MSG)

In the course of doing what you feel is necessary, what you determine is necessary becomes easy. Irrespective of your schedule, you can consciously choose to pray, study the word, tell others about Christ, become an example of Godliness, commit to service, and do whatever is necessary to maximize the grace of God upon your life.

Faith is not by donation. It is by use. When you commit and take active steps, you find the provisions of Jehovah-Jireh ('in the mount of the Lord it shall be provided' Genesis 22:14 ESV). You can take steps to increase your faith by making clear commitments to God in every area of your life.

21

THE TECHNOLOGY OF FAITH

Mountains are still moving today, if we get the technology right. There is a 'technology of faith'.

> Now in the morning, as they passed by, they saw the fig tree dried up from the roots. And Peter, remembering, said to Him, "Rabbi, look! The fig tree which You cursed has withered away." So Jesus answered and said to them, "Have faith in God. For assuredly, I say to you, whoever says to this mountain, 'Be removed and be cast into the sea,' and does not doubt in his heart, but believes that those things he says will be done, he will have whatever he says. (Mark 11:20–23 NKJV)

The day before, Jesus had seen from afar a fig tree having leaves and hoped to find fruits on it. He found nothing but leaves. The Bible also noted that it was not the season of figs. Still, Jesus cursed the fig tree. 'Let no man eat fruit from you ever again.' And His disciples heard it.

Peter, bewildered, remembered the events of the previous day and pointed out to the master that the tree He cursed had withered away.

> So Jesus answered and said to them, 'Have faith in God. For assuredly, I say to you, whoever says to this mountain, 'Be removed and be cast into the sea', and does not doubt in his heart, but believes that those things he says will be done, he will have whatever he says. Therefore

> I say to you, whatever things you ask when you pray, believe that you receive them and you will have them. (Mark 11:22–24 NKJV)

Jesus, at different instances, preached about faith, but this was the first time He told his disciples directly to 'have faith in God'. Faith makes us flexible for God's use. Contrary to a popular saying, our faith does not move God.

When we ask in prayer, we get a totality of what we ask. Asking without belief implies automatically that our unbelief is equally granted us when we do not receive what we ask. David's experience on return to Ziklag after the invasion by the Amalekites teaches us a worthy lesson in faith. Though distraught and despite his men considering stoning him, David encouraged himself in the Lord.

He demonstrated great faith. He did not despair or doubt God's ability to deliver him from his predicament; he believed God's delivering power. A child of God who involves God from the onset will end up praising Him with a testimony.

What does it take to have faith?

> Now this is the confidence we have in Him, that if we ask according to His will, He hears us. And if we know that He hears us, whatever we ask, we know that we have the petitions that we have asked of him. (1 John 5:14–15 NKJV)

Confidence to ask of God comes from asking according to his will. When we get our asking right, we will all have the same testimony Jesus had in Mark 11:22–24.

A man living in sin should not be at liberty to ask for prosperity from God. He should pray for sanctification. God's goodness leads to repentance. When a man genuinely enjoys the love of God, he will not bask in sin.

> Or do you despise the riches of His goodness, forbearance, and longsuffering, not knowing that the

goodness of God leads you to repentance. (Romans 2:4 NKJV)

God's will is not burdensome; it is good. It is His will that we prosper and be in health even as our souls prosper. God is still in the business of answering prayers, but prior to the prayers, our relationship with Him is paramount. Whenever we stand praying, we must be aligned to him.

Finally, Jesus said, "And whenever you stand praying, if you have anything against anyone, forgive him, that your Father in heaven may also forgive your trespasses" (Mark 11:25 NKJV)

Faith in God also means forgiving—not just those who offend us but also those who we have wronged.

> Therefore if you bring your gift to the altar, and there remember that your brother has something against you, leave your gift there before the altar, and go your way. First be reconciled to your brother, and then come and offer your gift. (Matthew 5:23 NKJV)

When we do these, we rightly align ourselves to God for mountains to move. The technology of faith is still very effective in moving mountains today.

22

FAITH IGNORES CIRCUMSTANCE

> Then one of the crowd answered and said, "Teacher, I brought You my son, who has a mute spirit. And wherever it seizes him, it throws him down; he foams at the mouth, gnashes his teeth, and becomes rigid. So I spoke to Your disciples, that they should cast it out, but they could not." He answered him and said, "O faithless generation, how long shall I be with you? How long shall I bear with you? Bring him to Me." (Mark 9:17–19 NKJV)

In the passage above, we understand that there was something the disciples were supposed to do but could not. The man who had the problem in this passage had been searching for the solution; the moment he saw Jesus, he ran to Him.

We also see that the disciples could not deliver the boy from this infirmity; the solution always lies with Jesus. Every other intermediary or messenger may fail; Jesus never fails. A messenger sent by God has a mandate to perform the instructions of God. However, if the messenger fails to bring about the desired result, we must realize it has nothing to do with the one who sent Him. Once you place your trust in Jesus, do not waver.

The Canaanite woman who came to Jesus for her daughter's healing showed great unwavering faith in spite of the opposition she encountered. This is recorded as follows:

> Then Jesus went out from there and departed to the region of Tyre and Sidon. ²² And behold, a woman of Canaan came from that region and cried out to Him, saying, "Have mercy on me, O Lord, Son of David! My daughter is severely demon-possessed." But He answered her not a word. And His disciples came and urged Him, saying, "Send her away, for she cries out after us." But He answered and said, "I was not sent except to the lost sheep of the house of Israel." Then she came and worshiped Him, saying, "Lord, help me!" But He answered and said, "It is not good to take the children's bread and throw it to the little dogs." And she said, "Yes, Lord, yet even the little dogs eat the crumbs which fall from their masters' table." Then Jesus answered and said to her, "O woman, great is your faith! Let it be to you as you desire." And her daughter was healed from that very hour." (Matthew 15:21–28 NKJV)

This woman was certain that this was the only authentic route to the delivery and restoration of her daughter. No matter what was thrown at her, she shrugged it off.

The man's attitude in bringing his son to Jesus irrespective of his previous experience with the disciples shows unwavering confidence in the ability of Jesus to heal the boy. Never get intimidated by your problem; God is more than sufficient to unravel it.

This principle is very important as people of faith. Faith is a journey. The road through faith has patience as one of its primary beacons. When you start the process of enjoying your deliverance from oppression or the process of reconciliation, you will be tempted to think that nothing is going on outwardly. Ensure you hang in there until you see the fulfilment of the promise of God.

The subject of the argument between the disciples and scribes was not recorded for us. But one issue is quite clear, whatever it was had to do with the inability of the disciples to cast out this foul spirit. It is possible that the scribes were mocking their inability to perform this miracle. But every controversy ended and arguments ceased the moment Jesus appeared on the scene.

We must approach God knowing and convinced that He alone is God. There is no alternative to Him, and, as Peter said, our attitude to Him must be based on the understanding that there is no alternative.

> But Simon Peter answered Him, "Lord, to whom shall we go? You have the words of eternal life." (John 6:68 NKJV)

The disciples asked Jesus a question; why could we not cast it out? His answer was simple: He said it is because of their unbelief.

Unbelief simply means not believing.

Faith does not negotiate with circumstances; it ignores it. Faith does not expose itself to negotiation. Those who trust God fully actually appear to be stupid at first; they have no motivation to argue. They have settled it in their hearts. You must regard the word of God as final. There is only one God!

Faith has only one picture: *it is well*!

Please notice something vital in our opening verse of scripture. It is recorded that the moment the boy was brought to Jesus, his situation appeared to worsen. This is recorded as follows:

> Then they brought him to Him. And when he saw Him, immediately the spirit convulsed him, and he fell on the ground and wallowed, foaming at the mouth. So He asked his father, "How long has this been happening to him?" And he said, "From childhood. 22 And often he has thrown him both into the fire and into the water to destroy him. But if You can do anything, have compassion on us and help us." (Mark 9:21–22 NKJV)

The first thing to notice and internalize is this, like the case of Lazarus that died when Jesus had said the sickness was not unto death, every problem that the devil initiates has the propensity to appear at its worst when the end is imminent.

> When Jesus heard that, He said, "This sickness is not unto death, but for the glory of God, that the Son of God may be glorified through it." (John 11:4 NKJV)

The boy's father said that this sickness and oppression had been on the boy since he was a child. If it was going to kill him, why had it not happened before the matter was brought to the attention of our Lord Jesus? This makes it clear to us that the life of a man is not in the hands of the devil or another man; it is in the hands of God.

The devil's game plan is to engineer the people of God to voluntarily give themselves up for destruction. This is what he tried to engineer when he caused Job's wife to advise him to curse God and die. His strategy is to bring the people of God to the point of self-pity; however, God does not give up on us. God's power has no measure.

23

CONTRARY TO EVIDENCE

One of the most revolutionizing features of our lives lately is the Internet. Though invisible, it affects our lives daily and drives the economy in various ways. We have radio signals and networks everywhere, indicating that the things we cannot see are more than what we can see.

It is also evident—as seen by international travel, cross-country e-commerce, cashless society, and so many other activities—that the world of the invisible is compelling the world to walk by faith. We have seen cases where different kinds of wind are responsible for aircrafts falling out of the sky or crash-landing at airports. How is it that the wind we can't see will bring down buildings and aircrafts we can see?

Isn't this contrary to the generally accepted worldly principle: seeing is believing? Evidence is seen as confirmation that something exists or has been paid for by the one in possession of the evidence.

We must understand that God has allowed the devil some space to operate in the world. It is one of those things we are unable to grasp at this time; maybe we will understand it in eternity. The devil is allowed to tamper with evidence, lie, and concoct many things. This is why Jesus told the Jews that they were of their father the devil, who lies out of his nature and resources.

The fact that every medical report state categorically that it is impossible for a woman to have a child does not make it truth. What they call hereditary disease/condition or curse does not have to get to you. They may have all the evidence, but truth resides in God only.

This explains why we often see events and information being propelled and galvanized in a particular direction; all evidence compelling us to believe that the outcome is certain. The fact that evidence points in a particular direction does not necessarily mean that it is the truth.

There was a case of a burglary in the UK, where the property owner's son travelled from the US to the UK and committed the crime. But he had left a meeting in the United States and so arranged his itinerary to take advantage of the time difference between the two countries that he entered a meeting with his doctor on return, and after that, his secretary.

The plot was so perfect that it would have been crazy to consider the man to be the culprit; his alibi was very strong. But what he didn't realize was that CCTV had been installed in the UK property and recorded his coming and going. The investigators worked from the truth to the evidence.

Before the CCTV footage was accessed and analysed, all evidence indicated that he had not committed the crime. I urge you to strive to progress from the truth to the evidence instead of concluding on the truth only by the evidence available.

In case you have drawn your conclusion based on the evidence before you, there is every possibility that you have believed a lie. Examine that evidence based on the word of God; if it is contrary to what God said, align yourself with the word of God. The word of God is truth.

> Now Israel loved Joseph more than all his children, because he was the son of his old age. Also he made him a tunic of many colors. But when his brothers saw that their father loved him more than all his brothers, they hated him and could not speak peaceably to him. Now Joseph had a dream, and he told it to his brothers; and they hated him even more. So he said to them, "Please hear this dream which I have dreamed: There we were, binding sheaves in the field. Then behold, my sheaf arose and also stood upright; and indeed your sheaves stood all around and bowed down to my sheaf." And his brothers said to him, "Shall you indeed reign over us? Or shall you indeed have dominion over us?" So they hated him even more for his dreams and for his words. (Genesis 37: 3–8 NKJV)

Joseph's brothers hated him immensely because of his dreams and his words, but more so because their father loved him. They said, 'Look, the dreamer,' meaning that the dream had swallowed his substance. Interestingly, we do not determine what we dream; our dreams are given to us. We must be able to dream from the word of God and speak concerning it; God will watch over the word to perform it.

You can kill a man and the dream continues to live on. It was the dream of Martin Luther King Jr that produced Obama as president of the United States. The source of the dream sustains the dream. The brothers of Joseph thought the dream would die if they killed Joseph. Little did they realize that God manipulates the heavens to help us; we must be zealous to open our mouths and boast of the Most High God.

It doesn't matter what I can present physically as evidence, as long as I know who is present in me. If you truly know that the creator of heaven and earth loves you, you will never walk with your head bowed down. Joseph was hated because of the love of his father; indeed, the devil hates us because God truly loves us. The capacity of God, who loves me, called me by my name and redeemed me from destruction, covers for everything.

The psalmist said he would make his boast in the Lord. If we keep our mouth shut, how can the heathen know God? Has God sent a word to you?

The Lord spoke the word concerning this land, Nigeria, to us, long before the advent of terrorism: the land is good. We are convinced that irrespective of what goes on here, we stand on this word knowing that the One who spoke the word is powerful enough to accomplish it.

That information is factually correct does not mean it is truth. If Job had the privilege of knowing that the devil took permission from God beforehand, he would have had fun in his experience. We should never face our challenges from the perspective that the devil is uncontrolled and arbitrary in his operations. The story of Job makes this clear to us; he of necessity needed to obtain permission from God.

In verse 31, we see that the brothers of Joseph took his coat and soaked it in blood, and on the basis of the evidence, Jacob concluded that Joseph had been slain, as he had been told.

> So they took Joseph's tunic, killed a kid of the goats, and dipped the tunic in the blood. Then they sent the

tunic of many colors, and they brought it to their father and said, "We have found this. Do you know whether it is your son's tunic or not?" And he recognized it and said, "It is my son's tunic. A wild beast has devoured him. Without doubt Joseph is torn to pieces." Then Jacob tore his clothes, put sackcloth on his waist, and mourned for his son many days. (Genesis 37:31–36 NKJV)

In conclusion, a few interesting questions arise from the scripture above. Was it Joseph's coat? Yes. Was there blood on it? Yes.

But was Joseph dead? No. Did a wild beast tear him? No.

The Lord is telling you that your natural analysis has come to a wrong conclusion. That the symptoms of an illness are there or that the physical conditions are present does not mean that it is truth. Please know this today, there is too much at stake for God to fail in your life.

We have several examples of men and women in scripture that dared to trust God instead of accepting the evidence before them: David, Daniel, Esther, and many more. God didn't fail them then. He cannot fail you now.

24

I Am Not Home Yet

> Let not your heart be troubled; you believe in God, believe also in Me. In My Father's house are many mansions; if it were not so, I would have told you. I go to prepare a place for you. And if I go and prepare a place for you, I will come again and receive you to Myself; that where I am, there you may be also. And where I go you know, and the way you know. (John 14:1–4 NKJV)

Home is a place where everything is prepared for you. While rounding up His ministry on earth, Jesus said to His disciples,

> "And if I go and prepare a place for you, I will come again and receive you to Myself; that where I am, there you may be also" (John 14:3 NKJV).

The Christian faith is so different from any other that making a comparison is quite derogatory. We are too far apart from the rest. The primary reason is because the hopes and aspirations of every human being we see or interact with here on earth, as long as they are not born again, terminate here on earth.

The apostle Paul, inspired by the Holy Ghost stated as follows,

> For if the dead do not rise, then Christ is not risen. And if Christ is not risen, your faith is futile; you are still in your sins! Then also those who have fallen asleep in

> Christ have perished. If in this life only we have hope in Christ, we are of all men the most pitiable. (1 Corinthians 15:16–19 NKJV)

The case of the believer is entirely different as expressed in the scripture above. How futile and awful a life lived without eternal consideration is bound to turn out. This explains why our Lord Jesus stated expressly, 'I go to prepare a place for you.' This means that, for the Christian, this world is not the prepared place; we are just passing through.

> Now on the first day of the week, very early in the morning, they, and certain other women with them, came to the tomb bringing the spices which they had prepared. But they found the stone rolled away from the tomb. Then they went in and did not find the body of the Lord Jesus. And it happened, as they were greatly perplexed about this, that behold, two men stood by them in shining garments. Then, as they were afraid and bowed their faces to the earth, they said to them, "Why do you seek the living among the dead? He is not here, but is risen! Remember how He spoke to you when He was still in Galilee, saying, 'The Son of Man must be delivered into the hands of sinful men, and be crucified, and the third day rise again.'" (Luke 24:1–7 NKJV)

We find in the passage above that when the women got to the tomb, the Angel said to them, 'Why do you seek the living among the dead?'

One great wish of the disciples and everyone who loved Jesus was for Him to establish His kingdom here on earth. But Jesus made it clear that it was expedient that He goes. Ironically, proponents of other faiths were trying to make this world a better place; Jesus stated clearly that everything we go through on earth is intended to prepare us for the 'hereafter'.

The events in the world would have caused our hearts and strengths to fail if not for the Word of God. There are many troubles in the world, but anytime I look into the word of God, I see answers to situations and challenges that I find troubling.

Christians the world over are overlooking the things that are important and giving attention to material and superficial things. We have become people whose only motivation is the acquisition of mansions and estates in this present world that our Lord Jesus made clear is not our destination.

Is it a wonder then that we are losing our young men and women to false religions, when all we present to them are matters of comfort and breakthrough on this side? We have failed to communicate the truth, and the vacuum we have created by this omission has enabled the proponents of the false religion to brainwash young people to blow themselves up in order to attain paradise. This is very sad and an indictment of every believer conscious of his faith in the world today. The only knowledge that can keep our young people safe is a clear understanding that there is eternity.

We have failed to communicate the true gospel of Jesus and inform the world that the Christian does not die; we sleep here and wake up on the other side. Jesus conquered death by going to the cross and resurrecting after three days. The sting of death was swallowed in victory. This world indeed is not our home, and the pursuit of earthly value is indeed chasing after the wind.

After the death and resurrection of Jesus; death became 'sleep' for the believer.

According to the scripture, in John 13:1–4, Jesus, knowing that, *God had given all things into His hands,* was not in doubt concerning His identity as the Son of God. He recognized himself not just as the first born of creation but as one who is together with the Father from the beginning. His statement at the point of betrayal by Judas buttresses this fact. The Bible records as follows:

> And suddenly, one of those who were with Jesus stretched out his hand and drew his sword, struck the servant of the high priest, and cut off his ear. But Jesus said to him, "Put your sword in its place, for all who take the sword will perish by the sword. Or do you think that I cannot now pray to My Father, and He will provide Me with more than twelve legions of angels? How then could the Scriptures be fulfilled, that it must happen thus?" (Matthew 26:51–54 NKJV)

A few chapters later, Jesus told His disciples as follows:

> And Jesus came and spoke to them, saying, "All authority has been given to Me in heaven and on earth." (Matthew 28:18 NKJV)

Indeed, there are many clear references to the fact that our Lord Jesus recognized clearly that the Father had delivered all things into His hands.

He Came from God, the Father

While at the home of Lazarus, our Lord Jesus made a declaration that was quite instructive and revealing. After the stone of unbelief was rolled away, He prayed as follows:

> Then they took away the stone from the place where the dead man was lying. And Jesus lifted up His eyes and said, "Father, I thank You that You have heard Me. And I know that You always hear Me, but because of the people who are standing by I said this, that they may believe that You sent Me. (John 11:41–42 NKJV)

A clear description of this understanding is provided for us by the first few verses of scripture, which introduced the gospel according to John, the apostle. It states as follows:

> In the beginning was the Word, and the Word was with God, and the Word was God. He was in the beginning with God. All things were made through Him, and without Him nothing was made that was made. In Him was life, and the life was the light of men. And the light shines in the darkness, and the darkness did not comprehend it. (John 1:1–5 NKJV)

He Was Going Back to God

Ultimately, he understood that as soon as His work here was done, that He would head back to where He came from. Before His crucifixion and subsequent resurrection, He stated as follows:

> These things I have spoken to you in figurative language; but the time is coming when I will no longer speak to you in figurative language, but I will tell you plainly about the Father. In that day you will ask in My name, and I do not say to you that I shall pray the Father for you; or the Father Himself loves you, because you have loved Me, and have believed that I came forth from God. I came forth from the Father and have come into the world. Again, I leave the world and go to the Father." His disciples said to Him, "See, now You are speaking plainly, and using no figure of speech! Now we are sure that You know all things, and have no need that anyone should question You. By this we believe that You came forth from God." (John 16:25–30 NKJV)

Be Like Jesus

When a believer knows where his faith comes from and the direction it is programmed to take him, every other thing falls into place. This revelation was what made Jesus roll up His sleeves to wash His disciples' feet.

The believer in Christ finds it easy to serve others, even his enemies, when such revelation is received. Remember that the apostle Paul admonished us as follows:

> Let this mind be in you which was also in Christ Jesus, who, being in the form of God, did not consider it robbery to be equal with God, but made Himself of no reputation, taking the form of a bondservant, and coming in the likeness of men. And being found in appearance

as a man, He humbled Himself and became obedient to the point of death, even the death of the cross. Therefore God also has highly exalted Him and given Him the name which is above every name, that at the name of Jesus every knee should bow, of those in heaven, and of those on earth, and of those under the earth, and that every tongue should confess that Jesus Christ is Lord, to the glory of God the Father. (Philippians 2:5–11 NKJV)

Our business here is to 'do business' and transact with whatever we have been given, whether an advantage or 'disadvantage', knowing that all things are working together for our good.

Is it not instructive that strangers always prosper more than the indigenes? It is hard to find a useless Yoruba man in an Igbo village. Their motivation is based on the understanding that their time is limited and must be utilized diligently. We must be about the Master's business with the diligence of a pilgrim. This is not our home. We do not belong here. We should have the mentality of foreigners and those on pilgrimage. We must wake up to this reality!

It does not matter how much you have or do not have. All that matters is His presence and the direction you are heading. This is not to say that we should become unfaithful in the responsibilities of our daily lives. We have to be conscious and certain that our pursuits are in the direction enlarging His kingdom here on earth; that is the agenda of heaven.

What our Lord Jesus delivered to us is far beyond our imagination, the Bible records as follows:

> Then I looked, and I heard the voice of many angels around the throne, the living creatures, and the elders; and the number of them was ten thousand times ten thousand, and thousands of thousands, saying with a loud voice: "Worthy is the Lamb who was slain To receive power and riches and wisdom, And strength and honor and glory and blessing!" (Revelation 5:11–12 NKJV)

It would, therefore, be unfortunate if your primary occupation and the focus of my faith is the acquisition of material things that are in passing, things that are subject to change, as scripture records:

> While we do not look at the things which are seen, but at the things which are not seen. For the things which are seen are temporary, but the things which are not seen are eternal. (2 Corinthians 4:18 NKJV)

The Bible's Easy-to-Read Version (*ERV*) presents the above scripture in clearer contemporary language:

> So we think about what we cannot see, not what we see. What we see lasts only a short time, and what we cannot see will last forever. (2 Corinthians 4:18 ERV)

Part Five

The Believer's Warfare

25

THE RIGHTS OF THE BELIEVER

> Then He spoke a parable to them, that men always ought to pray and not lose heart, saying: "There was in a certain city a judge who did not fear God nor regard man. Now there was a widow in that city; and she came to him, saying, 'Get justice for me from my adversary.' And he would not for a while; but afterward he said within himself, 'Though I do not fear God nor regard man, yet because this widow troubles me I will avenge her, lest by her continual coming she weary me.'" (Luke 18:1–5 NKJV)

If you have believed God and patiently waited for His salvation, then you realize the danger of giving up when the situation begins to appear hopeless. Sometimes, as the waiting period stretches, we tend to become distracted and forget the critical necessity of continuing in prayer.

In order to highlight the importance of this essential and critical fact—that it is necessary for men to consistently pray and never quit—Jesus told a story of a wicked judge who neither feared God nor had regard for any man. A widow came to implore him to intervene and save her from an adversary stronger than her.

It is important to note that the original intent of this story is not to compare the characters in the story to God and man. Our God is kind, merciful, and loving. Scripture tells us,

> For God so loved the world that He gave His only begotten Son." (John 3:16 NKJV)

The purpose of the parable is to emphasize the importance of not relenting in the place of prayer.

So in this story, we find a widow who was helpless and had no one to speak up for her before the judge. Rather than die in her predicament, she knew better to go to the judge for help.

Although he continuously refused her request, the story records that she persisted in her petition, saying to him,

> Get justice for me from my adversary. (Luke 18:3 NKJV)

She was unrelenting until he became weary of her and granted her request.

There are several lessons we can learn from this story:

Know Your Rights

> For my people are destroyed because of lack of knowledge. (Hosea 4:6 NKJV)

This widow recognized her rights were being violated and cried out for help. As a believer, you must know what your rights are in God in order to understand when they are being violated.

> There is an evil which I have seen under the sun, as an error … I have seen servants upon horses, and princes walking as servants upon the earth. (Ecclesiastes 10:6–7 KJV)

If you do not recognize what your rights are, you may continue unduly in the hardship derived from that ignorance. When you come to the realization that your situation is contrary to the promises of God, it is wisdom to prayerfully confront the situation.

In fact, the first line of prayer is coming to the conviction that a situation is contrary to the will and purpose of God. This knowledge places you on a pedestal and provides you the potential to change it. When you understand that you have rights in God and what those rights are, no undue situation will linger in your life.

Recognize the Source of Your Rights

How did you get the rights? Enforcement of rights is difficult when the enforcer is unaware of the source, authority, integrity and validity of the law or proclamation being implemented. Our Lord Jesus Christ gave us the right to son-ship:

> For as many as received Him to them He gave rights to become sons of God. (John 1:12 KJV)

The moment you submit your life to Christ, heaven recognizes you and takes responsibility for your well-being. This is truth you must believe, confess, and live in order to walk in its reality.

Friends, when you truly understand the price Jesus paid on the cross, you will surely reject any infringement on your derived rights.

So, if you are a child of God, do not panic unnecessarily at challenges. Jesus has given you dominion over sin, sickness, disease, marital, monetary problems, etc.

In every area of your life, you should expect to excel and bear fruits of excellence to glorify God. The price has been paid in full.

Know Your Adversary

Who is your adversary? The correct identification of the real enemy will eradicate the confusion that has enveloped the world and expedite the process of solution. Your adversary is not that old woman or old man in your village. In fact, when we begin to battle the wrong persons, we ruin our fight as believers. It can be likened to a football team leaving the scheduled location for a football match for another location. They will lose the match without even playing.

The adversary is the devil; although he has agents, yet he remains the main enemy. We must realize that we are in a war where the enemy is constantly raging to *steal, kill,* and *destroy us* (John 10:10).

Therefore, we must decide that he will not gain a foothold or an upper hand over our lives. The Bible admonishes us as follows:

> Be sober; be vigilant; because your adversary the devil, as a roaring lion, walks about, seeking whom he may devour. (1 Peter 5:8 KJV)

Know Your Avenger

Who else but God can help you? When you truly realize your solution is in God alone and nowhere else, it becomes easier to anchor steadfastly in Him no matter the challenge or turbulence.

The widow came continuously to the Judge to avenge her, but he would not. That, however, did not deter her. She kept coming back until she wearied him.

Friends, God is your deliverer. He alone can bless and change that situation; there is salvation in no other.

So do not be weary. Say, like Simon Peter,

> Lord, to whom shall we go? You have the words of eternal life. (John 6:68 KJV)

It is wisdom to wait patiently on the Lord, for surely, in due time, that request will be granted. We have established that these rights have been given because the Son of God, Jesus Christ, came into this world and paid the ultimate price. This price is designed to enable the believer walk in victory. The believer, therefore, must know his rights, recognize the source of these rights, and know who the real enemy is as well as His Avenger.

> Being confident of this very thing, that he which hath begun a good work in you will perform [it] until the day of Jesus Christ. (Philippians 1:6 KJV)

26

THE NECESSITY OF CONFRONTATION

Confrontation refers to a hostile situation or challenging contest between two opposing parties. Every real champion must be challenged at some point. The onus lies on him to assert and reinforce his position by defeating the challenger, if he intends to retain his prime position. In fact, before you can be regarded as a professional, you must have had a number of amateur contests.

> So the LORD God said to the serpent: "Because you have done this, You are cursed more than all cattle, And more than every beast of the field; On your belly you shall go, And you shall eat dust All the days of your life. And I will put enmity Between you and the woman, And between your seed and her Seed; He shall bruise your head, And you shall bruise His heel." (Genesis 3:14–15 NKJV)

An unceasing battle was declared in this bible passage above; it has been a running battle whose origin lies in the events surrounding the fall of Adam and Eve in the garden of Eden. This war rages between the agenda of God and the agenda of Satan. It is a battle that has been won by our Lord Jesus, but that victory must be enforced whenever and wherever it dares to be contested.

We understand and believe that God created all things by His Word, as recorded for us in the beginning:

> In the beginning God created the heavens and the earth. (Genesis 1:1 NKJV)

This is the only true God and every attempt to project any other requires that such intransigence be confronted and addressed. The God who started all things from the beginning is almighty, omnipotent, omniscient, and He is the one who will wrap it all up, as stated in the book of Revelation.

The adversary has never hidden his desire for worship, and over time, he has deceived men and women to regard him beyond his very estate. It is a believer's duty to address these anomalies by confronting them and enforcing the truth.

We know and understand what the Word of God states regarding our lives and the magnitude of victory that Jesus delivered to us. All that Jesus did was for us, to bring us back to the design and purpose of the Father. It is therefore unfortunate when we let matters He delivered into our hands slide into the hand of the adversary. We know what His word says about healing and what His stripes mean to us, as scripture states,

> Who Himself bore our sins in His own body on the tree, that we, having died to sins, might live for righteousness—by whose stripes you were healed. (1 Peter 2:24 NKJV)

Knowing this requires that we enforce this reality in the face of every attack of sickness and disease. It is a huge compromise if we knowingly let this slide because we are afraid of confrontation.

> He shall bruise your head, And you shall bruise His heel. (Genesis 3:15 NKJV)

For too long, we have been wary of exposing our heels to the serpent's bruise. Consequently, opportunities to bruise his head have been missed at every turn.

It is good that we maintain peace since that is an integral part of our call. The apostle Paul, writing in Hebrews, said,

> Pursue peace with all people, and holiness, without which no one will see the Lord. (Hebrews 12:14 NKJV)

However, there are situations and circumstances where confrontation becomes inevitable. Whatever tries to malign God, who created all things, must be confronted and brought to alignment. No one should look to find God when you are there.

> Then the seventy returned with joy, saying, "Lord, even the demons are subject to us in Your name." And He said to them, "I saw Satan fall like lightning from heaven. Behold, I give you the authority to trample on serpents and scorpions, and over all the power of the enemy, and nothing shall by any means hurt you. Nevertheless do not rejoice in this, that the spirits are subject to you, but rather rejoice because your names are written in heaven." (Luke 10:17–20 NKJV)

As the disciples returned from their journey, they came to Jesus and shared their excitement on their success in casting out demons. Jesus told them that the greater matter to celebrate is having their names written in heaven.

This is a worthy celebration and the basis for the authority necessary for any confrontation on His behalf. Having your name written in heaven places you at a vantage position to enforce the rule of God in our environment.

I have come to realize that spiritual people hardly understand the interplay between the physical manifestations and the spiritual factors. The way the spiritual person should fight is different from the way the world fights.

The disciples actually went into the Gentile nations to preach the gospel and cast out demons. It was Jesus who sent them and gave them the mandate to perform as they subsequently did. The necessary fight is to discover the mind of God regarding any situation and align with it. Our Lord Jesus was apparently telling them to rejoice that their names are written in heaven rather than rejoicing the fact that the demons were subject to them. By inference, once your name is written in heaven, the demons are subject to you.

27

THE WEAPONS OF OUR WARFARE

As we have been learning and observing, the Christian journey or life is warfare, and we must never lose sight of this fact. It is very important that we remind ourselves of what is at stake. We did not start the war, but we have become enlisted in it.

But I am compelled to ask at this time if you truly understand the issues at the heart of the struggle. What sort of fight is it, and what is at stake? What is the strategy of the enemy? What are we fighting for and what are we defending? Is it our finances, families, joy, welfare, or honour? What is the enemy really after in my life?

The Bible asks a pertinent question:

> For what will it profit a man if he gains the whole world, and loses his own soul? (Mark 8:36 NKJV)

This verse of scripture begins to answer the question for us; it points us in the direction of realizing that the battle on earth is for the souls of men.

For a Christian, the first level of this battle is the understanding that the adversary is eager to seize his soul. Since a person cannot deliver another while bound himself, being bound essentially truncates all that God could have used him to accomplish. Our mission is to keep ourselves and do damage to his kingdom through the deliverance of souls already bound.

Clearly, the battle lines are ultimately defined. But how do we fight? Ephesians 6:10 says,

> Finally, my brethren, be strong in the Lord and in the power of His might. Put on the whole armor of God, that you may be able to stand against the wiles of the devil. For we do not wrestle against flesh and blood, but against principalities, against powers, against the rulers of the darkness of this age, against spiritual hosts of wickedness in the heavenly places. Therefore take up the whole armor of God, that you may be able to withstand in the evil day, and having done all, to stand. Stand therefore, having girded your waist with truth, having put on the breastplate of righteousness, and having shod your feet with the preparation of the gospel of peace; above all, taking the shield of faith with which you will be able to quench all the fiery darts of the wicked one. And take the helmet of salvation, and the sword of the Spirit, which is the word of God; praying always with all prayer and supplication in the Spirit, being watchful to this end with all perseverance and supplication for all the saints. (Ephesians 6:10–18 NKJV)

Amazingly, the scripture above, which some scholars refer to as the strategy for spiritual warfare, begins with 'finally'. It is interesting that the admonishment before 'finally' had very natural and deliberate counsel. It mentions daily things like employees serving their masters truthfully and fairly and children being obedient to their parents. This suggests to us that the vital elements of spiritual warfare involve our daily choices.

> Bondservants, be obedient to those who are your masters according to the flesh, with fear and trembling, in sincerity of heart, as to Christ; not with eyeservice, as men-pleasers, but as bondservants of Christ, doing the will of God from the heart, with goodwill doing service, as to the Lord, and not to men, knowing that whatever good anyone does, he will receive the same from the Lord, whether he is a slave or free. And you, masters, do the same things to them, giving up threatening, knowing

> that your own Master also is in heaven, and there is no partiality with Him. (Ephesians 6:5–9 NKJV)

This notable warfare strategy advises you to 'put on the whole armour of God' that you 'may' be able to withstand the wiles of the devil. This makes it clear that God has provided the armour for me to put on. This armour was made for me to withstand the strategy of the enemy. The strategy of the enemy is peculiar to each person. It is not based on strength. He does not overcome us with raw power; he uses tricks and deception instead.

In terms of power, there is no contention between God and the adversary. At the mention of the name of Jesus, every knee will bend.

There is no contention as it regards power: *God created the devil.* The enemy simply uses cunning deception. For instance, he can reveal someone's weakness to me, intending that I judge that person and get caught up in the sin of pride.

Fighting our battles successfully requires that we take sides with the word of God. That is the only safe place where the enemy cannot reach.

Whenever you take a position on any matter based on any reason other than truth; you have sided the devil.

We are advised to put on the whole armour of God, complete gear in all ramifications. So there is a part for us to play in this warfare that we are enlisted; a lot depends on us. Our war is not against people. We are at war with one who fights by decoy, tricks, and subterfuge.

> For we do not wrestle against flesh and blood, but against principalities, against powers, against the rulers of the darkness of this age, against spiritual hosts of wickedness in the heavenly places. (Ephesians 6:12 NKJV)

When Daniel was praying, he was called greatly beloved based on his standing on righteousness. There was great contention over Daniel and heaven had to send reinforcement. We must be careful to make a point of standing right at all times.

Every Nigerian who is a Christian must be aware that because of God's agenda, there is a fierce battle over the soul of our nation. If the believers in our nation can stand at the place Jesus prepared for them, on truth, we will really bruise the head of the enemy.

The Bible says, 'Stand therefore, having girded your waist with truth.' Truth is the word of God. It is truth whether I like it or not. It is constant.

The girdle of the Roman soldier is what holds together the whole of his dressing, including his sword; that's what was used in the scripture to depict truth. Without the girdle, the soldier would be naked.

> For the weapons of our warfare are not carnal but mighty in God for pulling down strongholds, casting down arguments and every high thing that exalts itself against the knowledge of God, bringing every thought into captivity to the obedience of Christ. (2 Corinthians 10:4–5 NKJV)

Once we hold on to truth, we are at liberty to put down the lies of the devil. Truth enables us to hold on to Jesus while discarding whatever is contrary.

If every Christian in Nigeria begins to war with truth, Nigeria will change overnight. We cannot make excuses based on our interest because truth is truth; it does not waver. It has integrity (wholeness).

If you believe in prosperity, you must believe in judgment and righteousness as contained and expressly stated in God's word. Truth is what you look at and take a dressing; we cannot look at truth and adjust it. When we look at it, it serves to reveal to us where we need realignment. May we never be involved in any attempt to bend the truth in any aspect of our lives.

28

WINNING YOUR BATTLES

There are many forms of war that have been fought in the history of mankind—the world wars, international wars, continental wars, regional wars, civil wars, tribal wars, family wars, marital wars, corporate wars, interpersonal wars (wars between individuals), as well as intrapersonal wars (i.e., wars that go on within the mind of an individual).

Interestingly, the wars that get the most attention are the external wars that attract and engender the greater influence. However, the victory on the larger or international scale will matter less if you lose your personal battle. No matter how great or decisive the victory of the Iraqi army over ISIS, it has very little to do with the welfare of the man battling a debilitating dependence on hard drugs in a remote part of Iraq.

The point is this: we must be careful not to be consumed by what is happening on a large scale and miss out on what is personal, internal and exclusive to us. Indeed, in our world today, there are threats of bombings, disease, air strikes, killings, stealing, kidnapping, corruption, and neglect of duty. So much is going on as regards politics—the rise of some nations as well as the collapse and devastation of others.

There is so much trouble on every side, but the scripture says,

> No temptation has overtaken you except such as is common to man; but God is faithful, who will not allow you to be tempted beyond what you are able, but with the temptation will also make the way of escape, that you may be able to bear it. (1 Corinthians 10:13 NKJV)

Therefore, what is the way of escape from the current disorder in our society?

As children of God, the first thing we must settle is that our God is still in control, no matter the situation. Our God, the Creator of the world, has not lost control. The earth was in a non-existent state, devoid of form, but God spoke life into it and pronounced the same earth 'good'. No matter how bad things get, there is *One* who can make it good, *One* not overwhelmed or intimidated by how bad things are.

The goal of the devil in the midst of the chaos is to make you and I think that God has lost control. His intent is for people to fall into the deception of trying to resolve the problems through his methods. This is the primary reason for the multiplication of vices in our society.

We give the devil victory and occasion for more disorder in our society when we think and act as if God has abandoned His creation.

Remember, when Jesus fed the multitude, there were only five loaves of bread and two fishes, which were definitely not enough for five thousand people (not counting women and children). He directed the people to sit down. The challenge you and I have is to sit still in the midst of trouble and refuse to be unnecessarily reactive to the things happening around us.

Many people are mean today because the world has been mean to them; the man extorting a bribe from people blames his superior for not crediting his account with his due allowances. The mob on the street executes jungle justice, which is in itself a crime for our lack of trust in the authorities. This doesn't help the situation; all it does is to shift your allegiance away from the government of God to that of your enemy—the devil—who is the author of all confusion.

However, standing still and knowing that God is still in control in the midst of chaos challenges you to inquire from God, what He would have you do in that situation.

The Bible makes it clear that as people of God, there are battles that are not ours but God's (2 Chronicles 20:15). It is not our place, as a Church body, to go to war against terrorists; it is God's battle to fight.

God took ownership of the battle after Jehoshaphat, and his people came to Him; He orchestrated events and turned their enemies against themselves. All they had to do was go into the enemy's camp and get the spoils of war.

It takes a revelation of the power of God for a politician who is a Christian to refuse rigging in an electoral system where rigging is virtually the order of the day. Otherwise, he will be stating that God does not have the power to give him victory over his opponent who rigged.

Any result that is obtained through the path of iniquity does not have God's backing; our deliverance will not come as a result of our striving. God said to Jehoshaphat, 'Position yourself.' There is a part of the battle that is not about your striving but about your obedience.

What killed Goliath was not necessarily David's stone; it was David's obedience and submission to the plan and purpose of God. David couldn't work with Saul's armour because he had not proved it. What is happening in our time is that those who are meant to be working with God now go into 'Saul's armory' to take weapons, protections, attitudes, and strategy to get into the *battle,* whereas what we ought to do is occupy ourselves with knowing the mind of God concerning the situation.

Exodus 12:1–12 buttresses the two cardinal points. There is a part of the battle that purely belongs to God and one that is based on our submission to the plan and purpose of God.

God was going to strike the firstborn of every house in Egypt. Note that He didn't say 'the firstborn in every Egyptian house'. The truth is that every firstborn of every house that did not have the blood on its doorpost died. If there was any Israelite who did not obey the command, surely his firstborn died because the rule was, 'If I see the blood, I will pass over' (Exodus 12:13 NKJV).

The emphasis here lies on 'individual responsibility'. Many of us are sick and tired of the problems in our society, but we sit back and analyse the responsibilities of the various sectors and where they have failed; but the Spirit is asking you to focus on how to bring about solutions in your sphere of influence.

God is still in control but will not interfere in your individual responsibility (battle) because it is a condition that you must fulfil. You cannot make it through the times we are in right now by analysis alone but by conscientiously doing what God requires of you. The times we live in should produce in us the most faithful husbands and wives, the most dependable stewards, the most reliable ministers, etc.

We cannot keep doing what God has told us not to do and also worry about terrorist activities and corrupt government officials. This *battle* is an individual charge to purification—the push for righteousness, purity, and sanctification.

We do not overcome the devil with physical weapons; we must go up against him putting on the whole armour of God (Ephesians 6:10–18). The scripture says, 'And having in a readiness to punish all disobedience, when your obedience is complete' (2 Corinthians 10:6). Hence, we must fulfil our own side of the battle, which is obedience to the will of God in every situation we find ourselves.

If you fail to win the personal battle, you cannot contribute meaningfully to the battle on the larger scale. There are battles you need to fight on the home front, in your workplace, in your relationship with people and your service to God, etc.

The Bible says *endure hardness as a good soldier of Christ* (2 Timothy 2:3). The mark of a good soldier is not necessarily his weapon but the discipline he exercises. Decide today that you will not lie, cheat, fornicate, steal, or be covetous. Determine to love and be faithful to your spouse, submissive to your parents, and faithful in your work place; this is your personal battle.

The same way every vehicle has a manufacturer; God is the manufacturer of the world. If it gets 'bad', we simply take it back to him for repairs. Fixing things in our own way can only lead to more frustration and catastrophes. God has not lost control; he remains steadfast in fulfilling His part of the equation, but we must fulfil ours in *righteousness* and quit worrying about what is going on outside of our battle zone. If everyone were determined to do what is expected of them according to the standard of God, the world would be a better place.

29

GOD'S LOVE IN ACTION

I have realized that the trickiest matters that result in our failures are not the complex things; they are actually the very simple issues. The simplicity of these facts, the fact that they appear basic and mundane, deceive us into overlooking them.

Scripture records that our Lord Jesus was emphatic in making reference to being childlike:

> At that time the disciples came to Jesus, saying, "Who then is greatest in the kingdom of heaven?" Then Jesus called a little child to Him, set him in the midst of them, and said, "Assuredly, I say to you, unless you are converted and become as little children, you will by no means enter the kingdom of heaven. Therefore whoever humbles himself as this little child is the greatest in the kingdom of heaven." (Matthew 18:1–4 NKJV)

This vital instruction is easy to overlook because it is so simple. Knowing human beings, we would have taken it more seriously, if it were something more demanding or tasking than this simple admonition. If, for instance, Jesus said, you cannot enter unless you fast forty days and nights, this would probably have become one of the cardinal teachings of Christianity and would be accorded great relevance.

When questioned on which of God's commandment was the greatest, Jesus replied,

> You shall love the LORD your God with all your heart, with all your soul, and with all your mind.' This is the first and great commandment. And the second is like it: 'You shall love your neighbor as yourself.' On these two commandments hang all the Law and the Prophets. (Matthew 22:36–40 NKJV)

Looking at children, it is easy to see why our Lord Jesus made the earlier reference regarding being converted to be like them. Their love and loyalty to God surpasses everything; and their love, friendship, and genuine care for each other is what God expects us to learn as adults. They mix completely, not mindful or respectful of any prejudices.

Our Lord Jesus said,

> He who has My commandments and keeps them, it is he who loves Me. And he who loves Me will be loved by My Father, and I will love him and manifest Myself to him. (John 14:21 NKJV)

This expresses and highlights the way God views love. Having the word/commandment is only one side; obedience or adherence to the word you have is the other side.

In other words, the love of the Father, which transcends His love of His creation, is conditional. His love for His creation is universal. Entering into the Father's love must be through the establishment and sustenance of a relationship—conformance is precedent to continued enjoyment.

The walk with God is quite simple and not complex. But it requires a clear understanding of the way things work. There is only one God and His creation. One side of that equation is strong, while the other is weak. One side of the equation is wise, while the other is foolish. God is the strong and wise One, while I am the weak and foolish one.

You are destined to have a smooth and delightful walk with God if you stand on this premise. God is the One who calls the shots, He is the originator, the One who started it and will also end it.

Some of the factors critical to being childlike are trust and obedience. Children are so trusting and obedient at different levels including their caregivers and parents. It is important we are truthful to the children so we do not lose their trust, thereby catalysing rebellion.

Also important is being mindful as adults of our conduct and behaviour because what they see is what they will do, not what you say. We must be consistent in reinforcing righteousness and be firm in reprimanding whenever necessary.

God is looking for children. He is not looking for old men and women already set in their ways, not malleable. To walk with God, you must be ready to be transformed by new light, adjusting to the image and stature of our Lord and Saviour Jesus Christ. This, in itself, is an exercise in spiritual warfare.

Children will not waste their time in bitterness, envy, jealousy, and all the other conditions that are inimical to your spiritual development. The purity of a child's heart passes the prayer purity test; let's not forget that every prayer is purified.

Like our Lord Jesus said, let us all be converted and be like little children so that we can enter into the kingdom of God. Let us humble ourselves like children so that we can be the greatest in the kingdom of God.

30

LOOKING THROUGH THE EYES OF THE CROSS

The apostle Paul had this to say in 1 Corinthians 2:1–5 (NKJV):

> And I, brethren, when I came to you, did not come with excellence of speech or of wisdom declaring to you the testimony of God. For I determined not to know anything among you except Jesus Christ and Him crucified. I was with you in weakness, in fear, and in much trembling. And my speech and my preaching were not with persuasive words of human wisdom, but in demonstration of the Spirit and of power, that your faith should not be in the wisdom of men but in the power of God.

Many believers have faith that rest on the wisdom of men. They do things the same way they see the world do them. The Bible says that the wisdom of God is foolishness to the world (1 Corinthians 1:21). You can have faith in so many things as well as anything; faith is confident expectation that what you believe will come to pass. Having faith is not the same thing as having faith in God.

Our Lord Jesus stated clearly that we should have faith in God. This is a different faith from the confident expectation in outcomes. The world will try to duplicate or compare the genuine faith in God with that of the world.

When Moses appeared before Pharaoh for the first time and performed the miracle of casting down his rod before Pharaoh, the magicians of Pharaoh also did the same. As it happened, the rod of Moses swallowed the rod of the magicians. When Faith is true and genuine, it will swallow up whatever seeks to counterfeit or contend with it.

Looking at our nation and the time we are in, I can see clearly that things will always happen; matters will always be at the front burner in life and society. A few weeks ago, it was the fuel scarcity. Then it was the removal of subsidy. Now it is about a woman beheaded in Kano.

Cast your mind back to the fear of the millennium bug in the run-up to the year 2000. Things keep happening and changing; some will make you happy, and others will make you sad. But realize that heaven is not mindful of most of what we have concerned and occupied ourselves with in life.

The real businessman will concern himself with his bottom line; how much profit is in the venture for him? Different individuals will have differing perspectives and interpretations from a singular incident, depending on their motivation. When you lose a dear one, it may be a family tragedy but a business opportunity for those in the casket making and allied business. So there is always varying perspectives in every situation.

Heaven has an interest. The apostle Paul said in 1 Corinthians 2:2 (NKJV), 'Determine not to know anything among you except Jesus Christ crucified.'

Meanwhile, Matthew 6:33 says, 'Seek ye first the kingdom.' It is all about the kingdom—not being distracted by things, needs, and deprivations of earthly value but being focused on heaven's purposes and plans. We must be careful to maintain the Christian 'worldview' in everything.

In view of the current turmoil and wickedness in our world, the hateful atrocities committed against innocent persons, can we find it in us to even love and pray for those who have wronged us, those we perceive as 'monsters'?

The Church must prod itself and return her focus to God. The hope of God, in all this, is that the world will find salvation by the spread of the Word through believers. He has come for all to be saved. Turnover defines how much activity has been generated, but does it always reflect true profit? No. The kingdom's desire is that all, not some, be saved.

Mark 15:18–32 recounts the crucifixion journey. The way of the Cross was a very difficult process for even His apostles to follow. How could God allow this? How could One so powerful let Himself be treated thus?

What is the difference? The way God approaches issues is different from that of men. We *must* view events and happenings from a different perspective. We *must* view through God's eyes.

God wants our vision to be coloured by the heavenly agenda. This path is so incredible—not every Christian understands or agrees with it. But by the renewal of our minds through Christ, it is possible. May the Holy Spirit quicken your Spirit to comprehend this truth, in Jesus's name!

The wisdom of God enables you to submit under the mighty hand of God. God is the 'exalter'. John 13:3–4 tells us how Jesus, our example, girded His loins with a towel and washed the feet of His disciples.

May we humble ourselves before God and receive from Him the ability to look through His eyes in Jesus's name!

31

THANKSGIVING IS A DUTY

The moment you realize the direction your life was heading before Jesus saved you, the battles He fought on your behalf, the natural and expected reaction of you is thanksgiving. We all owed debts whose penalty was death. Nothing and no one was found worthy to break the bonds with which we were bound so we could be free.

In the book of Revelation, this graphic scenario is laid out for us as follows:

> Then I saw a scroll in the right hand of the one sitting on the throne. The scroll had writing on both sides and was kept closed with seven seals. And I saw a powerful angel, who called in a loud voice, "Who is worthy to break the seals and open the scroll?" But there was no one in heaven or on earth or under the earth who could open the scroll or look inside it. I cried and cried because there was no one who was worthy to open the scroll or look inside. But one of the elders said to me, "Don't cry! The Lion from the tribe of Judah has won the victory. He is David's descendant. He is able to open the scroll and its seven seals." Revelation 5:1–5 (ERV)

The right understanding of redemption can only provoke gratitude and loyalty. When we consider the totality of what Jesus has accomplished for us, the natural response is to give Him worthy praise.

As we appear in Church regularly, looking splendid, as we all do, if we recall that we would have been dragging different kinds of animals to this place of worship as was provided in the old covenant, we would all be humbled.

Some would have come with cows, he-goats, turtledoves, pigeons, and so many other creatures, depending on the magnitude of what was committed. On arrival at the place of sacrifice, a priest would carefully examine the animal to ensure it was free of any blemish. It could be sacrificed only if it was certified by the priest; yet that animal had no power to cleanse the sin totally. It only covered it.

This ultimate sacrifice of the Son of God provides us great privilege, but where there is such privilege, there is also great temptation. It becomes easy to take everything for granted when the love God has for us is considered. It's easy for us to think everything is about us, forgetting that we were created for God's pleasure; we are essentially creatures of pleasure.

Praise is comely or fitting in the lips of the righteous as stated in the book of Psalm:

> Rejoice in the LORD, O you righteous! For praise from the upright is beautiful. (Psalm 33:1 NKJV)

This means that it is the right and proper thing for the saved to praise God with the understanding of what God has done for them. Our praise must be total and unconditional; everything that has breath should give God praise.

As believers, we must understand that God is very jealous and takes it personally when we place anything before or higher than Him. We are in warfare, and the enemy is doing all he can to keep us perpetually in negativity, should we give him room. Our adversary will seek to orchestrate false events that try to pressure us into disobeying God. His tools are numerous, and he works negatively to encourage us in self-indulgence and pride.

Some Christians are passionate about several things. Some watch football as leisure, while to others, it's a religion. Some believers will not identify with Jesus as a brand but are quick to praise and even go out on a limb for their teams. They pay no attention to the things of God but are beside themselves with joy or sorrow based on the fortunes of their teams or the state of their passions. Their excitement for these things surpass their allegiance to God and His agenda. What a wasteful misplacement of priority.

Some think that because they are educated and enlightened they shouldn't be beside themselves for God; this is the lie of the devil. King David understood that it's not about who he was as king; rather, it was more about where God brought him from to the palace. He carefully and deliberately made it clear to Michal that considering where God brought him from; it was very fitting for him to uncover himself and dance like a commoner before God.

Clearly, if every born again Christian understood where God brought them from, that He saved them from eternal damnation and has made them kings and priests unto God, they would have no other attitude except of gratitude to God and speaking to one another in psalms, hymns, and spiritual songs.

> Speaking to one another in psalms and hymns and spiritual songs, singing and making melody in your heart to the Lord. (Ephesians 5:19 NKJV)

Indeed, as scripture puts it,

> For when we were still without strength, in due time Christ died for the ungodly. For scarcely for a righteous man will one die; yet perhaps for a good man someone would even dare to die. But God demonstrates His own love toward us, in that while we were still sinners, Christ died for us. Much more then, having now been justified by His blood, we shall be saved from wrath through Him. For if when we were enemies we were reconciled to God through the death of His Son, much more, having been reconciled, we shall be saved by His life. And not only that, but we also rejoice in God through our Lord Jesus Christ, through whom we have now received the reconciliation. (Romans 5:6–11 NKJV)

May the Lord enable us to walk worthy of the call we have been called by being profitable servants of the Most High God.

Conclusion

If you prayerfully read this book and invested time in meditating on its contents, I promise you that your life will never be the same, in the name of Jesus!

I started out letting you know what it means to give God first place, how to follow His leading with attentiveness and diligence, no matter how inconvenient it may seem.

Also, I believe you have come to understand that your future is certain, since there is an end intended and expected for every child of God. God created you with a purpose in mind; you are not here on earth by accident.

It is important that you are aware that none of this will be possible if you fail to depend on Him and practice what you learn through His word and the leading of His Spirit daily.

These will equip you to fight a good fight and enforce the victory that our Lord and Saviour Jesus Christ won for us on Calvary.

I will end this book reminding you of this scripture:

> Then a voice came from the throne, saying, "Praise our God, all you His servants and those who fear Him, both small and great!" And I heard, as it were, the voice of a great multitude, as the sound of many waters and as the sound of mighty thunderings, saying, "Alleluia! For the Lord God Omnipotent reigns! Let us be glad and rejoice and give Him glory, for the marriage of the Lamb has come, and His wife has made herself ready." (Revelation 19:5–7 NKJV)

Our God reigns forever and ever! He is the One who started all things! He is still in charge! *He* will wrap it all up when *His* purpose has been accomplished!

May all glory and honour be unto Him in the Mighty Name of *Jesus*! *Amen*!

About the Author

Ikenna Okeke is the senior pastor of The Father's Church, a vibrant assembly of believers with headquarters at Eden Centre, Abuja.

He is a remarkable, insightful, and practical teacher of the word of God whose message has enabled many people to find hope and restoration through Jesus Christ.

His answer to God's call in 1997 to 'go to Abuja and raise Me men that I can use' is born out of his unyielding passion, dedication, and love of God. Blessed with a unique teaching gift, Pastor Ikenna delivers insightful messages on the development of the total man are well received across various platforms, such as radio, television, and online social media.

He began his early ministry as pioneer pastor at the Desire of Nations Parish of the Redeemed Christian Church of God, Abuja. He served in that capacity for six years before a proceeding call of God led him to the establishment of The Father's Church, in November 2003.

A chartered accountant by training, he obtained a bachelor of science degree in accounting from the University of Nigeria and served in various capacities in the banking industry before this call.

Pastor Ikenna is a man with a proven heart for God, a tender heart for God's people, and a deep passion for righteous living.

He is married to Pastor Chineze Okeke, and they are blessed with two children.

Lightning Source UK Ltd.
Milton Keynes UK
UKHW042303250719
346752UK00008B/95/P

9 781728 389615